D1603525

MARTIN LUTHER'S
CHRISTOLOGY AND ETHICS

MARTIN LUTHER'S
CHRISTOLOGY AND ETHICS

Dietmar Lage

Texts and Studies in Religion
Volume 45

The Edwin Mellen Press
Lewiston/Queenston/Lampeter

Library of Congress Cataloging-in-Publication Data

Lage, Dietmar.
   Martin Luther's Christology and ethics / Dietmar Lage.
      p.   cm. -- (Texts and studies in religion ; v. 45)
   Includes bibliographical references.
   ISBN 0-88946-834-6
   1. Luther, Martin, 1483-1546--Contributions in Christology.
2. Luther, Martin, 1483-1546--Ethics. 3. Identification (Religion) -
-History of doctrines--16th century. 4. Jesus Christ--History of
doctrines--16th century. 5. Christian ethics--History--16th
century. I. Title. II. Series: Texts and studies in religion ;
45.
BR333.L27 1990
230'.41'092--dc20   89-77128
                                             CIP

This is volume 45 in the continuing series
Texts and Studies in Religion
Volume 45 ISBN 0-88946-834-6
TSR Series ISBN 0-88946-976-8

A CIP catalog record for this book
is available from the British Library.

The Edwin Mellen Press   The Edwin Mellen Press
Box 450   Box 67
Lewiston, New York   Queenston, Ontario
USA 14092   CANADA L0S 1L0

The Edwin Mellen Press, Ltd.
Lampeter, Dyfed, Wales
UNITED KINGDOM SA48 7DY

Printed in the United States of America

To Jeanette --

for her many good works

CONTENTS

***

ABBREVIATIONS

WA   *D. Martin Luthers Werke, Kritische Gesamtausgabe* (Weimar, 1883 ff.) Vols. 1 ff.

References include volume and page numbers.

WA Tr.   *Tischreden* (Weimar Ausgabe, 1912 ff.)

References include volume and page numbers.

WA Br.   *Briefwechsel* (Weimar Ausgabe, 1930 ff.)

References include correspondence numbers.

LW   *Luther's Works* (U.S.A.: Concordia Publishing House and Fortress Press, 1955 ff.) Vols. 1 ff.

References include volume and page numbers.

PREFACE

Slightly more than five hundred years have passed since the birth of Martin Luther. During this period, thousands of volumes have been published helping us to understand his life and thought. However, only recently has Luther scholarship broken free of denominational influences and agendas. Protestant scholars are now free to be critical of Luther and appreciative of the medieval traditions which gave rise to his thought. Catholic scholars are now free to be appreciative of Luther and critical of the late medieval traditions he attempted to reform. This is a new era in Luther scholarship -- one in which criticism and appreciation can work together to give us a more accurate understanding of both Luther and his late medieval context. This work consciously tries to situate itself within this new era of Luther scholarship.

As all historians know, historical development, whether on a social or personal level, occurs as the result of many and diverse influences. However, as one moves through life, the influence that others have had is often not clearly recognized until many miles and years have elapsed and a critical distance attained.

The task of writing an acknowledgment presents a welcome opportunity to reflect on one's life in order to assess the influence of others and express appreciation. The greatest possible influence that others can exert is in initiating and shaping one's continuing interests.

My initial interest in the history of Christianity was recognized by Dr. Victor E. Peters of Westgate Mennonite Collegiate (Winnipeg, Manitoba). An enthusiasm for historical theology was fostered by Dr. H. Gordon Harland (Manitoba). Dr. J. Arthur Boorman (McGill) stimulated my interest in theological ethics. I am indebted to Dr. Joseph C. McLelland (McGill) for instilling an appreciation of the continuing need to study the reformation period. My concentrated interest in Luther was evoked by Dr. Douglas J. Hall (McGill) under whose direction this work first began to take form. I gratefully acknowledge their continuing influence in shaping my academic interests.

I am also indebted to Ms. Barbara Reaburn and Mr. Sean Moriarty of the University of Windsor Computer Centre, whose acumen with word processing equipment contributed significantly to this work.

Most of all, I am grateful for my caring, faithful critic, Jeanette N. Marshall to whom this work is dedicated.

University of Windsor   *D. L.*

INTRODUCTION

After reviewing a number of secondary works which have made valuable contributions to our understanding of the thought of Martin Luther, Joseph Lortz observes that most studies deal primarily with the theology of the so-called 'mature' Luther. Still others focus on particular writings. However, few attempt to trace specific themes throughout the twists and turns of Luther's continual development. Lortz concludes: "It is startling, but we actually do not have detailed investigations of Luther's major theological concepts that would trace these concepts continuously through all of his vast writings."[1]

One of the obstacles in attempting a detailed investigation of Luther's major theological concepts encountered by the historian is Luther himself. It may seem almost trite to point out that Luther was not a systematic theologian or dogmatician, yet it remains true nevertheless and should not be lost sight of in any analysis of Luther's thought.[2] Luther's major theological concepts were rarely clearly defined and even when a concise definition can be approximated, Luther moves on, always restlessly wrestling with theology. While it is not true that one can find justification for almost any position in Luther's writings, one can find the sources for a number of quite diverse positions.[3] This lack of a systematic approach combined with Luther's continual change and development makes it nearly impossible to speak in terms of 'the theology of Martin Luther.' Indeed this is so little possible as attempting to sketch a bird on the wing. One

Introduction

can speak of Luther's thought only in reference to a particular time and narrowly-defined set of circumstances, for Luther was above all a product of, and always responsive to, his particular environment. This realization has led to an increasing awareness among historians that a proper understanding of even his confessional writings is impossible without taking account of the particular stage of his development and other ideational currents prevalent within the late medieval and early reformation context.

Of all histories, the history of ideas may be the most elusive. Ideas exert a powerful force on human affairs, but a force difficult to estimate, for unlike tangible items, ideas cannot be weighed, measured or otherwise empirically verified. This inability to approach objectively the study of the impact of ideas on an historical period points to another problem encountered by the historian. To be more specific, as Gordon Rupp has pointed out, one of the difficulties of historical research is that of assuming that themes which are fundamental to our age had a similar importance in the past.[4] To approach historical materials with the intent of illuminating contemporary concerns runs the risk of distorting the past by elevating in stature themes which may have been considered minor at the time. The search for relevance may threaten an accurate understanding of a period with permanent concealment under the silt of historical investigation. On the other hand, themes which may appear to be of peripheral importance to our age may have been highly significant in the past and can provide us with an important clue to a proper understanding of specific thinkers or of the period. One such theme which finds expression in all of the late medieval and early reformation movements, which, however, has been almost entirely overlooked in Luther studies, is the *imitatio Christi*.

The imitation of Christ, having been a dominant motif of much of Christian ethics from the time of Jesus to the present, holds a venerable position in the history of Christian thought. Throughout the Middle Ages the *imitatio Christi* served not only an ethical significance but provided a soteriological function as well. For many Protestants, and Lutherans in particular, the imitation of Christ is so inextricably intertwined with the pre-reformation period that any mention of the imitation of Christ cannot help but evoke images of late medieval Roman Catholic mysticism and asceticism with which it was so closely associated.

The reformation is often viewed as a time of new beginnings rather than as the continuation of a faith originating centuries earlier. The differences rather than the similarities with the older tradition are stressed. Protestants often believe, particularly in terms of the tradition of the imitation of Christ, that Luther ended the tradition rather than reforming it.

Many distinguished theologians, historians and scholars, including Regin Prenter,[5] Gustaf Wingren,[6] Olavi Tarvainen,[7] Gerhard Rost[8] and Lennart Pinomaa,[9] among others, take the position that Martin Luther rejected the *imitatio Christi* in his rejection of much of late medieval Roman Catholic doctrinal theology. Many arguments are made in support of this interpretation of Luther's position in regard to the imitation of Christ.

Lennart Pinomaa, focusing upon Luther's doctrine of works in comparison to late medieval doctrines, argues that Luther rejected the *imitatio Christi* as part of his rejection of the scholastic doctrine of works with its claims to righteousness, meritoriousness and soteriological efficacy.[10]

Olavi Tarvainen acknowledges that originally there may have been a continuing presence of the *imitatio Christi* in Luther's thought, but at the same time he argues that after his break with scholasticism, the 'mature' Luther rejected

3

Introduction

the *imitatio Christi* and replaced it with his Christ-mysticism and *conformitas Christi*.[11]

Both Regin Prenter and Gustav Wingren believe that the *imitatio Christi* is grounded in the mystics' assumption of an innate unifying anthropological, generic or volitional link between human nature and God. According to them, this is a denial of the creature/Creator distinction and is incompatible with Luther's understanding of the true nature of sin and *sola fide, sola gratia*.[12]

Pinomaa and Tarvainen both take the position that the doctrine of *imitatio Christi* is dependent upon a late medieval and radical reformation Christological formulation which Luther rejected.[13]

Pinomaa and Wingren take the stance that the *imitatio Christi* suggests a slavish, literal, and legalistic mimicry which denies human freedom, creativity and the conscience. It restricts the Christian's ability to act responsibly in the real world. It is therefore incompatible with Luther's doctrine of vocation and represents a denial of a truly moral life.[14] Closely related to this view is the belief that the *imitatio Christi* is derived from a literalistic interpretation of Scripture and in light of contemporary Biblical criticism no clear picture of the historical Jesus exists for Christians to imitate.[15]

This last point is the most problematic for the contemporary mind. Imitation means mimicry; obedience means slavery. However, Luther must be understood within the context of his late medieval milieu. Within this context obedience meant freedom not slavery; and the imitation of Christ, properly understood, meant the ability to live a moral life. Luther clearly rejected mimicry or 'aping,' as he referred to it, just as he rejected the so-called 'third use of the law,' but he did not reject the guidance and direction offered to Christians by Christ's example.

This work attempts to respond to the arguments noted above which claim that Luther rejected the imitation of Christ as incompatible with other major elements of his thought. It will be shown that although Luther criticized much of the late medieval understanding of the *imitatio Christi*, this was done in order to reform the concept rather than as a rejection of it. It will also be demonstrated that Luther retained the *imitatio* motif, not only accidentally, as a subconscious holdover from an earlier stage of his development, but consciously, as an essential and necessary component of his thought, integrally related to his other major Christological and ethical themes throughout the various stages of their development.

In contrast to the position of Tarvainen, this work will show that the *imitatio* appears not only in the 'young' Luther but in the so-called 'mature' Luther as well. The *imitatio* was not replaced by Luther's Christ-mysticism and *conformitas Christi* as claimed, but was retained in conjunction with these essential Christological themes. While it is true that *conformitas Christi* replaced the *imitatio Christi* in terms of soteriological significance, the *imitatio* retains its historic significance in the realm of morality.

This work will also show that although Luther rejected any claims of righteousness, meritoriousness and soteriological significance associated with the imitation of Christ, he did not reject the *imitatio* as he did not reject the law. Luther's theological ethics required that Christians perform good works and the *imitatio Christi* is maintained to provide guidance and direction for those works to be performed.

It is true, admittedly, that the *imitatio Christi*, as understood by most medieval traditions, is rooted in the notion of an inherent link between human nature and God, and as such Prenter and Wingren are correct in their assertion that the *imitatio* is incompatible with Luther's doctrines of sin, faith and grace. However, while Luther consistently emphasized the Creator/creature distinction, he also maintained that Christ was given to the faithful as both a gift and an example. Christ's function as *exemplum* is maintained despite the fact that his function as *sacramentum* is the only soteriologically significant Christological reality -- and Luther's primary concern was always soteriology.

It is also true, as stated by Pinomaa and Tarvainen, that the *imitatio Christi* is dependent upon an Augustinian *sacramentum et exemplum* Christological

Introduction

formulation. However, as will be shown, Luther did not reject this Augustinian formula as claimed. What Luther rejected was the preeminence granted to the *exemplum* in medieval thought. In that soteriology was his primary concern, his emphasis on the *sacramentum* is understandable, but not to the exclusion of the *exemplum* as claimed by both Pinomaa and Tarvainen. As will be shown, Luther's Christological 'breakthrough' lay in reformulating the Augustinian Christology, not in rejecting it.

While the theme of the imitation of Christ is the specific theme to be addressed in this work, it should already be quite apparent that this is only possible against the backdrop of the larger themes of Luther's Christology and his doctrine of works.

An overriding concern of this work, however, is that of challenging the particular underlying methodological assumptions by which many historians approach Luther. It is the position of this work that the generalized viewpoint -- that Luther was radically different from the late medieval traditions which preceded him and the other reform traditions which accompanied him -- tends to lead historians to approach individual themes within Luther's thought in terms of antithetical categories. The emphasis is on a discontinuity between Luther and his context rather than on continuity. This work, in tracing the classical medieval theme of the imitation of Christ throughout the twists and turns of Luther's career, attempts to show that Luther was not as radically different from the traditions which preceded him, nor for that matter from the other reformation traditions, as is so often assumed.

NOTES

1. Joseph Lortz, "The Basic Element of Luther's Intellectual Style," in *Catholic Scholars Dialogue with Luther*, ed. Jared Wicks (Chicago: Loyola University Press, 1970), p. 4.

2. Jaroslov Pelikan, *From Luther to Kierkegaard: A Study in the History of Theology* (Saint Louis: Concordia, 1950), p. 25.

3. Ian D. K. Siggins, *Martin Luther's Doctrine of Christ* (New Haven: Yale University Press, 1970), p. XXII.

4. Gordon Rupp, "Word and Spirit in the First Years of the Reformation," *Archiv für Reformationsgeschichte*, 49 (1958), p. 13.

5. Regin Prenter, *Spiritus Creator: Luther's Concept of the Holy Spirit*, trans. John M. Jensen (Philadelphia: Muhlenberg Press, 1953), see esp. pp. 8-13, 50-61, 145ff., 179ff., 210-219, 252ff.; see also "Luther's Theology of the Cross," *Lutheran World*, 6 (1959), esp. pp. 222-233. Reprinted as *Luther's Theology of the Cross* (Philadelphia, 1971), pp. 1-24.

6. Gustaf Wingren, *The Christian's Calling: Luther on Vocation*, trans. C. C. Rasmussen (Philadelphia: Muhlenberg Press, 1957), see esp. pp. 171-184; see also "The Christian's Calling According to Luther," *Augustana Quarterly*, 21 (1942), pp. 3-16; and "Was bedeutet die Nachfolge Christi in evangelischer Ethik?," *Theologische Literaturzeitung*, 75 (1950).

7. Olavi Tarvainen, "Der Gedanke der *Conformitas Christi* in Luthers Theologie," *Zeitschrift für Systematische Theologie*, 22 (1950), see pp. 26-43.

8. Gerhard Rost, "Der Gedanke der Gleichformigkeit mit dem lebenden Christus in der Frömmigkeit des jungen Luthers," *Lutherischer Rundblick*, 11 (1963), see pp. 2-12.

9. Lennart Pinomaa, *Faith Victorious: An Introduction to Luther's Theology*, trans. Walter J. Kukkonen (Philadelphia: Fortress Press, 1963), see esp. pp. 48, 57-58, 81, 108, 158, 172-174, 177.

10. See Pinomaa, pp. 57-58, 177.

11. See Tarvainen, pp. 26-43; Prenter, *Spiritus Creator*, pp. 25-26; Rost, pp. 2-12; and Pinomaa, p. 95.

12. See Prenter, *Spiritus Creator*, p. 51; and Wingren, *Christian's Calling*, pp. 8, 172.

13. See Pinomaa, pp. 48, 81; and Tarvainen, p. 34.

14. See Pinomaa, pp. 108, 158, 172-174, 177; and Wingren, *Christian's Calling*, pp. 172, 181, 233.

Introduction

15. This final point will be dealt with only inferentially. The medieval mind understood Scriptural discrepancies as the result of a failure of ability on the part of the reader rather than as an inconsistency within Scripture. The purpose of this work is essentially historical in nature, and this objective precludes asking questions of Luther which do not arise in his frame of reference.

I. THE STATE OF LATE MEDIEVAL SCHOLASTICISM

A. *Via Antiqua, Via Moderna*

- 1 -

The primary framework of theological consciousness in central Europe at the turn of the sixteenth century was provided by the waning, yet still considerable, influence of scholasticism. Contemporary scholasticism was no longer marked, if indeed it ever truly had been, by a singular, unitary theological approach. The scholastic synthesis, having broken into factions, was in a state of decline. Successive Church Councils, guided by the spirit of the Conciliar Movement, officially recognized the plurality of theological approaches as having valid foundations in tradition and thus legitimized and enhanced them.

While it is admittedly difficult to characterize and delineate clearly the various branches of the scholastic movement, two major theological traditions can be discerned. The lineages of these factions can be respectively traced to the thought of two Oxford-educated Franciscan contemporaries. The 'realist' (*reales*) tradition, or the *via antiqua*, as it came to be known, originated with 'the subtle Doctor,' John Duns Scotus (c. 1265-1308). The *via moderna* or 'nominalist' (*nominales, terministae*) tradition had its source in the thought of William of Ockham (c. 1285-1347).[1]

In that both *viae* were branches of scholasticism, both were similar in regard to many of their basic theological presuppositions. There were,

The State of Late Medieval Scholasticism

nevertheless, significant differences between them, both in terms of emphasis and theological substance. Before turning to those aspects which make them unique, it may be of value to examine some of their shared characteristics.

- 2 -

Following Thomas Aquinas (1225-1274), the various branches of late medieval scholasticism conceived of grace as 'a certain supernatural thing in man coming into existence from God.'[2] There was general agreement between the *viae* that grace was granted by God as a reward for the performance of works or acts which were deemed by God to be meritorious in nature (*actum meritorium*) and deserving of a reward. Included among these meritorious acts were prayer, giving to the poor, celibacy and fasting, as well as many others. The Christian, having received an infusion of grace (*infusio gratiae*), is disposed toward God and the performance of meritorious acts. The Christian, in co-operation with God's grace, engages in works for which a further infusion of grace is granted as a reward. The more good works one performs, the more merit and grace one receives. This enables the performance of still more good works. Within this context of *cooperari*, progressive righteousness could be achieved by human initiative and preserved by means of practise (*habitus*), similar to learning to master the playing of a musical instrument. By means of the habit of performing good works, even though the intention and motivation to do them may not be naturally present within the agent, eventually the proper feelings and intentions would be generated. Ultimately, once enough merit has been established and righteousness has been ingrained as a habit of the mind, the final reward, graciously granted by God to the faithful, is salvation.

Both scholastic *viae* shared this common soteriological methodology and generally agreed upon the necessity of its various components, including *cooperari*, the *actum meritorium*, the *infusio gratiae* and *habitus*. There were,

10

nevertheless, subtle yet significant differences in their respective understanding of the specific nature and function of these concepts.

- 3 -

Central to the process of co-operating with grace in order to receive a further infusion of grace and attain progressive righteousness was the performance of works deemed meritorious by God. While the promise of the reward of righteousness and salvation no doubt provided the adherents with the necessary impetus and motivation to perform works, intentionality, while always a prerequisite for good works, is not by itself sufficient. It still remains, especially for scholastic methodology, that one must know the good that is to be done. It is in their response to this epistemological requirement that the *viae* differed markedly.[3]

For the *via antiqua* tradition, which was closely aligned with Thomistic thought in this regard, the good is revealed in the natural law (*lex naturalis*). Natural law, in turn, has been established by the one universal and eternal God. It follows therefore that the good must have a universal and eternal nature. What is good today will be good tomorrow; what is good in one context will also be good in another context. This *a priori* nature of the good manifested in the natural law is readily discernible and knowable by all by means of reason (*rationis*).[4]

William of Ockham rejected this notion of the good as universal. In fact, he rejected universals entirely, arguing that these are solely mental constructs rather than having a metaphysical, transcendent reality in and of themselves.[5] For Ockham, the belief in the inherent certainty of reason as a means by which the good is known had resulted in layers of canonized metaphysical speculation, obfuscating and distorting the reality of primary experience rather than providing a true understanding of the good. Instead, Ockham emphasized the transient and mutable nature of the good.

For William of Ockham, God cannot be trapped by universals. The good is whatever God ordains. However, God has absolute power (*potentia Dei absoluta*) and is therefore free to change radically the nature of the good. Furthermore, if God is free and able to change the good, it follows naturally that humanity as well must have radical freedom of the will in order to be able to conform to the changing will of God. Without this ability, the entire concept of co-operating with God and the *actum meritorium*, which were so central to all elements of the scholastic enterprise, would be threatened. In placing the stress upon a free will, both that of creature and Creator, Ockham was attempting to purge contemporary Christianity of the fatalism and determinism which he saw as the medieval legacy of predestinarian tendencies inherited from Saint Augustine.

Ockham's rejection of universals as mental constructs and metaphysical speculation led him to criticize and ultimately reject another significant feature of contemporary scholasticism -- namely its understanding of the nature of the self. According to both Thomas Aquinas and John Duns Scotus, natural law exists universally, and humanity, as a participant in this universal reality, has an innate or inherent understanding of the good. This innate understanding of the good has its source in an uncorrupted state or condition of human nature referred to as the *synteresis*.[6]

- 4 -

The *synteresis* is best understood as a refinement of the *imago Dei* tradition. Its roots run deep in the history of Christian doctrinal theology, playing a particularly significant role in the debates over the second person of the Trinity and theology of creation of the Patristic period. The *imago Dei* affirms that

12

humanity is created in the image of God, an image which had been distorted by the Fall. Although humanity has been corrupted, the Fall did not obliterate all vestiges of its pre-fallen Adamic purity. The indelible image of God continues to glow like a tiny spark in the hidden depths of the soul. For the Cistercian Abbot, Bernard of Clairvaux (1090-1153), the sinful soul is compared to an unfaithful spouse. The return to the bed of matrimony is possible because the *imago Dei* is present within the *synteresis*. The soul "preserves even in the region of unlikeness its inborn resemblance to God -- a manifest sign of its divine origins."[7] The *synteresis* is regarded as an autonomously functioning faculty given to humanity in creation which provides the self with both an inborn ability and an inherent disposition toward performing good works.

Thomas Aquinas and John Duns Scotus closely identified the *synteresis* with the intellective and cognitive functioning of the mind or reason, forming what may best be understood as a rational soul.[8] Morally correct acts must also be rationally correct acts. As Thomas Aquinas explains, "the *synteresis* is ... the law of our mind ..., a habit containing the precepts of the natural law, which are the first principles of human actions."[9] Knowledge of the good and the primary principles of morality which are contained within the natural law are indelibly imprinted upon the *synteresis*. The *synteresis* in turn informs the reason (*rationis*), and thereby determines human actions. Self-evident, infallible, universal and unalterable principles of action have been promulgated by God and instilled into the mind so as to be known 'naturally.'[10] The *synteresis rationis*, as it came to be known in the *via antiqua*, not only provided the self with an inborn understanding of God and the good, but also provided the self with a fixed disposition toward doing the good and obeying the precepts of natural law by means of the dictates of right reason.

William of Ockham considered the *synteresis* as another example of a mental construct having no reality in and of itself. The *synteresis* was another example of metaphysical speculation which he believed had been wrongly introduced into Christian theology from Greek philosophic sources (Plato). Just as doctrines of Divine omnipotence and freedom could not be safeguarded without eliminating the metaphysical presuppositions of universals, human freedom cannot be maintained in conjunction with a metaphysic of innate 'essences' which determine action.

Employing his famous so-called 'razor,' Ockham held that all concepts that are not absolutely necessary and not properly grounded in experience must be rejected as speculative metaphysical constructs.[11]   On this basis, Ockhamists and radical nominalists from Ockham onward generally rejected the *synteresis* with its fixed disposition toward doing good as a doctrinal threat to a proper understanding of free will.[12] Late medieval nominalism was distinguished by its insistence that humanity's relationship to God is not ontological, based on sharing necessary connections or a common nature. Rather it is based on voluntarily conforming our will to the will of God.[13]

- 5 -

Ockham's rejection of *a priori* universals and essences such as the *synteresis* led to a significant difference in the epistemology of the two *viae*. For Thomas Aquinas and John Duns Scotus, knowledge of the mind of God is openly available to all by means of the *synteresis rationis*.   For William of Ockham, however, without the metaphysical underpinning provided by the hypothetical *synteresis*, the *ratio* is reduced to the status of a limited epistemological tool rather than an innate connection between the self and God. For Ockham, reason is limited and should be relied upon only in the realm of nature.[14]   In its place Ockham stressed the function of revelation, intuition and experience as the means by which the will of God is known at a particular time and place. In opposition to Scotus, Ockham argued that the human condition is not characterized by a lack of knowledge of the good, but a failure of the will

14

to do the good. Humanity lacks a volitional or affective conformity to the will of the Divine.

Ockham's epistemological critique and rejection of the *synteresis* had the resultant effect of shifting the locus of morality from the reason to the will (*volunta*). For Ockham, it was the will that lay at the centre of the moral life. This shift to the will was not without its own difficulties.

While both *viae* agreed that righteousness could be attained by means of meritorious acts performed in co-operation with infused grace, there was some disagreement concerning the prior need of grace for the performance of meritorious works. The *via antiqua* emphasized that an infusion of grace by God was a necessary prerequisite for the performance of good works (*meritum de condigno*) while the *via moderna*, with its emphasis on a free will, regarded the *infusio gratiae* as a reward fitting to the deed for good works voluntarily initiated by the faithful (*meritum de congruo*).

Similarly, both *viae* accepted the Aristotelian concept of *habitus* with its emphasis on the ability to take on a new or second nature through habit, or more accurately, practise.[15] The *habitus* provided the rationale and underpinning of the belief in the elevation and perfectibility of human nature in its quest for holiness. However, while the *via antiqua* tradition argued that this second nature is bestowed as a gift of grace (*habitus infusus*), the *via moderna* emphasized the role played by the self in attaining this new nature (*habitus acquisitus*).

In attempting to defend their free will doctrine, nominalists were ultimately forced to claim that it was possible to do good works and attain righteousness without the prior need of an infusion of grace. As a result, they faced the official condemnation of the Church.

Epistemological questions concerning the good were generally considered as being legitimately within the realm of philosophical and ethical dispute. However, the questions raised by an understanding of the good as transient and mutable were perceived as an Ockhamist tendency to exaggerate God's arbitrariness and capriciousness. Later Ockhamists and nominalists, particularly

The State of Late Medieval Scholasticism

those at the University of Paris, were severely criticized by Church Councils which had been called to end the Great Schism (1378-1417). They were chastised for entering into subtle and useless philosophical disputations. These were considered as especially dangerous to ethics and they were exhorted to keep to the texts of the Fathers.

B. Gabriel Biel

- 1 -

Although there was official condemnation of some basic Ockhamist principles,[16] in general the *via moderna* movement was tolerated and growing in strength throughout central Europe. Many universities maintained both traditions side by side within their theological faculties, providing chairs for representatives of both traditions. What may be seen by some as a *confusio opinionum* was less pronounced at the University of Erfurt. It was the prerogative of the Elector of a district to determine which theology or combination of theologies would be taught at the universities within their jurisdiction. Erfurt (along with Vienna) was among the few universities which by decree were exclusively nominalist.

So pervasive and pronounced were the influences of the various branches of the medieval enterprise upon one another that it is difficult to speak of the respective *viae* as monolithic movements in their own right. Nominalism in particular was characterized by its diversity of expression.[17] While still falling under the influence of its *venerabilis inceptor*, the nominalism at Erfurt was shaped as much by Gabriel Biel, Jean Gerson, Peter d'Ailly, Gregory of Rimini, Johannes von Wesel and Martin Luther's teachers, Bartholomäus Arnold von Usingen and Jodocus Trutvetter, as it was by Ockham.[18] While not radically

16

Occamisti, the school was nevertheless recognizably a member of the *via moderna* tradition.

The primary Ockhamist influence on the faculty at Erfurt, and thus indirectly upon the young Martin Luther, came from Gabriel Biel (c. 1420-1495). Biel was a former member of the theological faculty at Erfurt (c. 1442, 1452) and as such was the teacher of Martin Luther's teachers. So significant was the influence of Biel and his particular form of nominalism that his adherents at Erfurt (and later Wittenberg) came to be known as *Gabrielistae*.

- 2 -

For the most part Biel was a nominalist. In several significant respects, however, Biel's approach is distinguished by his attempt to find a compromise among specific aspects of the *via antiqua* and *via moderna* traditions. Biel was sensitive to the official Church criticism leveled against the Ockhamist tendency to stress the arbitrary nature of the will of God or the good. This tendency was blamed for depreciating if not obliterating the basis for Christian ethics and morality. Biel sought a compromise which would preserve the basic Ockhamist tenets of God's omnipotence and freedom, as well as human freedom, while also ensuring that the will of God can be both known and accomplished by the faithful.

The first part of Biel's compromise consisted of a defence of Ockhamism. In support of the Ockhamist belief in a free will, Biel reinterpreted the *actum meritorium* doctrine, inserting the decidedly Ockhamist conditional clause 'freely chosen by the will.' Biel writes, "A meritorious act is an act freely chosen by the will and accepted (by God) for the granting of a reward."[19] In defense of the Ockhamist thesis concerning the transient and mutable nature of the good, Biel argues that the obligation of all Christians to do their best to live a moral life and to 'love God above all else' (*diligere Deum super omnia*), despite the changeable

17

nature of the good, remained. God helps those who voluntarily do their best. According to Biel, "God does not deny grace to one who does his best."[20] In fact, God infallibly and perhaps even necessarily grants grace to those who freely choose to do their best (*Deus infallibiliter gratiam dat*).[21]

The second aspect of Biel's compromise consisted of a concession to Thomism and the *via antiqua*. Ockhamist epistemology stressed experience, intuition and revelation as the means by which the changing will of God is known at a particular time and place. The problem is not so much one of knowing the will of God but of willing to act on the basis of this knowledge. Consequently, the locus of morality for Ockhamists came to be centred upon the will or *volunta*, while for Thomists and the *via antiqua* tradition the emphasis was placed upon the cognitive and intellective capacity of the *synteresis rationis*. Biel, recognizing that the heart and mind are both required for any morally good act, came to believe that the *synteresis rationis* and *voluntatis* are not necessarily mutually exclusive. In fact, it is not only necessary to know the good but also to will that the good be done. Biel broke with long-standing Ockhamist tradition and reintroduced the *synteresis*. The *synteresis* provides the basis for true wisdom, and only wisdom can lead to an increase of the charity which alone provides the basis for ultimate union with the Divine. Both the cognitive and emotional sides of human nature are informed by the *synteresis*. Biel's compromise, therefore, emphasized a double or twofold *synteresis voluntatis et rationis*.

While his reintroduction of the *synteresis* may appear to be a rather decisive concession to the *via antiqua*, Biel was also sensitive to the Ockhamist charge that the *synteresis*, if understood as a faculty of the mind providing a fixed disposition toward doing the good, was a doctrinal threat to the freedom of the will. Biel responded in two ways. In the first case, Biel redefined the *synteresis* using a concept borrowed from Germanic mystical theology. He argued that the *synteresis* should not be defined as a faculty of the mind which by its very nature compels the self to do good works. Rather it should be seen as an

18

'inextinguishable spark' or infallible moral knowledge and ability which inclines and "directs in general toward a just and right activity."[22]

This slight redefinition of the function of the *synteresis* in itself obviously does not solve Biel's problem. The other aspect of Biel's solution was his relocation of the *synteresis*. Biel argued that rather than being associated with the rational soul, the *synteresis voluntatis et rationis* must be seen to be located within the conscience (*scintilla conscientiae*), thereby serving the self in an advisory capacity.[23] By means of the *synteresis*, the conscience is made aware of the will of God or the good. Although it is always a sin to act against conscience (*contra conscientiam agere peccatum*),[24] the individual does retain the ultimate freedom to disregard the advice presented by the conscience. The individual is free and able to choose ignorance over wisdom and malice over charity. However, if the advice of the *synteresis*-informed conscience is followed, the self is guided and directed in its good works toward a harmony or conformity of will and reason with the Divine (*conformitas voluntatis et rationis Dei*).[25]

Biel emphasized that the *synteresis* should not be understood as a faculty of the mind providing a fixed disposition. Rather it should be seen as an inherent function or innate ability given to the self in its Adamic purity. In thus maintaining the *synteresis* as an ability rather than as a faculty, and in associating it with the conscience rather than the rational soul, Biel had successfully preserved the basic Ockhamist tenet of a free will and excluded the deterministic *necessitas* motif which had characterized the *via antiqua* tradition.

Nevertheless, it still remains that whether the *synteresis* is understood as a faculty or 'inextinguishable spark' or whether it is understood as providing a 'fixed disposition' or 'general inclination' toward good, just and right activity, the *synteresis* in both Biel and the *via antiqua* tradition provides an inborn moral consciousness. For both Biel and the *via antiqua* tradition, the *synteresis* provides an anthropological basis for ethical activity, representing a point of contact or natural covenant between the human and Divine. The first stage of meritorious action is grounded in the agent's natural reason and a will that is capable of heeding right reason. For Biel, the moral life and its good works remain based upon 'doing what is in one' -- *actum facientis quod in se est (facere quod in se est)*.

- 3 -

For Gabriel Biel, the Christian life consists of the continuous habit of righteousness in co operation with grace until one is eventually worthy enough to be granted the ultimate reward of salvation. Given the soteriological implications of Biel's understanding of the *synteresis*, *habitus* and *cooperarii*, the significant question to be addressed is that of the nature and function of Biel's Christology.

The primary focus of Biel's Christology, as it was for his entire age, was on the archetypal and paradigmatic nature of the life, work and death of Christ -- the *Christus exemplum*. Although the *synteresis* informs the conscience and directs the self to obeying the will of God, it is in the example of Christ that the will of God for humanity is fully revealed for all to see. While having been revealed, however, the work originating with Christ has not yet been fully accomplished. It still awaits completion.

Christ's death was understood by Biel as the inevitable culmination of a life of active obedience (*obedientia activa*) and perseverance in righteousness. Biel sees Christ's perseverance in righteousness, in life and in death, as humanity's most significant *actum meritorium*. Indeed, Christ's voluntary sacrificial death was so meritorious that the surplus merit it accumulated led God to grant all humanity an undeserved infusion of grace. While Biel acknowledges the efficacious validity of Christ's sacrifice and expiatory death, the *Christus sacramentum* nevertheless plays only a minor and restricted role. Biel limits the efficaciousness of the sacrifice by making it applicable only to original sin (*peccatum originale*).

20

Although by means of his suffering and death Christ has opened the gates to the kingdom for us, his work is not complete. The work originating with Christ awaits completion by means of our own *obedientia activa* in imitation of the example of Christ. In fact, as Biel maintains, "If we do not add our merits to those of Christ, the merits of Christ will not only be insufficient but non-existent."[26] Humanity has a free will. However, because of this freedom the intention of Christ's life and work can be frustrated by our failure to carry on that work. Christian meritorious works performed in imitation of Christ must complement the work originating with Christ. These meritorious works, to which the self is already directed by the *synteresis* and aided by grace, progressively conform one to the mind and will of God until eventually one is regarded as deserving of salvation.

NOTES

1. For an analysis of anterior theological traditions which culminated in the thought of Scotus and Ockham see Gordon Leff, *Medieval Thought from St. Augustine to Ockham* (Baltimore: Penguin Books, 1958) and Etiénne Gilson, *A History of Christian Philosophy in the Middle Ages* (New York: Random House, 1955), *passim.*

2. Thomas Aquinas, *Summa Theologica*, I-II, quest. 109-112; see also Frederick C. Copleston, *Aquinas* (Great Britain: Penguin Books, 1955), *passim.*

3. See Etiénne Gilson, *Reason and Revelation in the Middle Ages* (New York: Scribner, 1938), pp. 32ff.

4. "Natural law is nothing else than the rational creature's participation in the eternal law," Thomas Aquinas, *Summa Theologica*, I-II, quest. 91, art. 2, in *Introduction to St. Thomas Aquinas*, ed. Anton C. Pegis (New York: Random / Modern Library, 1948), p. 618; cf. John Duns Scotus, *De Primo Principio*, ed. and trans. E. Roche (New York: Franciscan Institute, 1949), esp. pp. 149-153.

5. Ockham, *Summa Totius Logicae*, in *Ockham: Philosophical Writings*, ed. and trans. P. Boehner (London: Thomas Nelson & Sons, 1957), esp. pp. 35-36;

see also Frederick C. Copleston, *A History of Philosophy* III, 1 (New York: Image Books, 1963), pp. 56-165.

6. The word is variously spelled as *synderesis, sinderesis, syneidesis, syntheresis.* For the sake of consistency, the spelling *synteresis* will be employed throughout.

7. Bernard, *Sermon* XXVII.6. Likeness to divinity is the beginning and end of humanity. "Cast out sin, the cause of this partial unlikeness and you will attain spiritual union, perfect vision and mutual love" (*Sermon* LXXXIII.4). The individual "Freed from sin will ... regain his rightful place by regaining his true likeness to the image of God which he bears within himself" (*Concerning Grace and Free Will,* X). Bernard's writings are available in numerous editions. See A. J. Luddy, *The Life and Teaching of St. Bernard* (Rep. of Ireland: M. H. Gill & Son Ltd., 1950).

8. See Heiko A. Oberman, *The Harvest of Medieval Theology: Gabriel Biel and Late Medieval Nominalism* (Mass.: Harvard University Press, 1963), p. 65.

9. Aquinas, *Summa Theologica,* I-II, quest. 94, art. 2 (Pegis edition), p. 636.

10. *Ibid.,* pp. 634-645, *et passim.*

11. Ockham, *Summa Totius Logicae* (Boehner edition), esp. pp. 92-95.

12. See Erwin Iserloh, "Nominalism: The Universities Between *Via Antiqua* and *Via Moderna,*" in *From the High Middle Ages to the Eve of the Reformation,* Vol. IV of the series *Handbook of Church History,* ed. Hubert Jedin and John Dolan (West Germany: Herder and Herder / Burns and Oates Ltd., 1970), pp. 334-355.

13. *non substantus confusos, sed voluntate consentaneos* -- see Gilson, *A History of Christian Philosophy in the Middle Ages,* p. 165; see also Steven Ozment, "Mysticism, Nominalism and Dissent," in *The Pursuit of Holiness in Late Medieval and Renaissance Religion: Papers from the University of Michigan Conference,* Vol. X of the series *Studies in Medieval and Reformation Thought,* ed. Charles Trinkhaus and Heiko A. Oberman (Leiden: E. J. Brill, 1974), p. 78.

14. Ockham, *Summa, loc. cit.*

15. The concept of *habitus* was derived from Aristotelian moral philosophy. Aristotle believed that moral virtues must be acquired through effort and practise. Although equipped naturally to become virtuous, one cannot really be virtuous except by performing virtuous acts. See Aristotle, *Nichomachean Ethics* 1103A-B in *The Basic Works of Aristotle,* ed. Richard McKeon (New York: Random

House/Modern Library, 1947), pp. 330-334. Thomas Aquinas followed Aristotle closely in this regard: "Man has a certain innate aptitude for virtue, but the perfection of virtue must accrue to him by discipline and training," *Summa Theologica*, I-II, quest. 95, art. 1 (Pegis edition), p. 647. For the influence of Aristotle on Aquinas see W. G. De Burgh, *The Legacy of the Ancient World* (Great Britain: Penguin Books, 1953), esp. pp. 436-463.

16. In 1326 Pope John XXII (1316-1334) stigmatized three of fifty-one selected Ockhamist theses as Pelagian. See Oberman, *The Harvest of Medieval Theology*, p. 325.

17. Heiko A. Oberman in "Some Notes on the Theology of Nominalism with Attention to its Relation to the Renaissance," *Harvard Theological Review*, 53 (1960), has identified four definable 'schools' within nominalism, pp. 47-76.

18. For a description of the Ockhamism of Luther's teachers, see Leif Crane's *Contra Gabrielem, Luthers Auseinandersetzung mit Gabriel Biel in der "Disputatio Contra Scholasticam"* (Kopenhagen: Gyldendal, 1962), pp. 9-41, and M. G. Baylor, *Action and Person: Conscience in Late Scholasticism and the Young Luther*, Vol. XX of the series *Studies in Medieval and Reformation Thought*, ed. Heiko A. Oberman (Leiden: E. J. Brill, 1977), pp. 118-120.

19. Gabriel Biel, *Collectorium circa quattuor libros sententiarum*, Lib. II dist. 27, art. 2, as quoted by Bengt Hägglund, "The Background of Luther's Doctrine of Justification in Late Medieval Theology," *Lutheran World*, 8 (1961), p. 30.

20. Biel, *Collectorium*, Lib. II, dist. 22, quest. 2, art. 3, as quoted by Hägglund, *op. cit.*, pp. 31-32.

21. Biel, *Collectorium*, Lib. II, dist. 28, art. 2, as quoted by Baylor, *Action and Person*, p. 279, n. 49.

22. See Biel, *Collectorium*, Lib. II, dist. 39, quest. 7, art. 2, concl. 1, as quoted by Walther von Loewenich, *Luther's Theology of the Cross* (Minneapolis: Augsburg Pub. House, 1976), p. 53.

23. This understanding of the *synteresis* as 'conscience' is a tradition reaching back to St. Jerome for whom the *synteresis* was "that spark of conscience which was not quenched even in the heart of Cain when he was driven from Paradise and by which ... we know that we sin." As quoted by Baylor, *Action and Person*, p. 26; see also David Knowles, *The Evolution of Medieval Thought* (New York, 1964), pp. 128-130.

24. A tradition reaching back to Abelard's *Ethica* -- see Baylor, *Action and Person*, p. 3; see also D. K. Frank, "Abelard as Imitator of Christ," *Viator:*

The State of Late Medieval Scholasticism

Medieval and Renaissance Studies, I, ed. L. White (University of California: Centre for Medieval and Renaissance Studies, 1971), *passim.*

25. For a discussion of Biel's twofold *conformitas voluntatis et rationis Dei*, see Oberman, *Harvest of Medieval Theology*, pp. 65-68.

26. As quoted by Oberman, *Harvest of Medieval Theology*, p. 268.

II. *CONTRA SCHOLASTICAM THEOLOGIAM*

A. Luther and Late Medieval Scholasticism

- 1 -

After receiving his *Baccalaureus Biblicus* from the University of Erfurt, the young Martin Luther was required by custom to lecture on the chief source book of medieval theology, Peter Lombard's *Four Books of Sentences*.[1] As his fragmentary notes indicate, the new *Sententiarius*[2] relied extensively upon Gabriel Biel's commentary, his *Collectorium circa quattuor libros sententiarum* (1501 edition).[3] Again, to underscore Biel's place within the Ockhamist tradition, it should be noted that his commentary was in itself a summary of William of Ockham's earlier commentary, *Quaestiones in quattuor libros sententiarum*, with several of Biel's own thoughts added.[4]

In 1508, Luther's teacher at Erfurt, Jodocus Trutvetter, received permission from the Elector to establish the *via moderna* in Wittenberg. He attempted in vain for two years but was not well received. Finally, in 1510, he was forced to return to Erfurt.[5] Three years later, Erfurt's newest graduate, Martin Luther, was sent to Wittenberg to represent the *via moderna*.[6] By August of 1513, the new Professor of Exegetical Theology began his first series of lectures on Psalms -- his *Dictata Super Psalterium*.[7]

The general biographical and circumstantial evidence indicates a close relationship between the young Luther, Gabriel Biel and the Ockhamist tradition.

Contra Scholasticam Theologiam

In fact, if we accept Luther's own evaluation, he did consider himself, philosophically at least, to be an Ockhamist during this period (1513-1516).[8]

In his early lectures and sermons, Luther reveals his own thought to be closely aligned to that of Biel. Luther maintains the *facere quod in se est*[9] and essentially the same twofold understanding of the *synteresis voluntatis et rationis* and *conformitas voluntatis et rationis Dei* as originally formulated by Biel.[10] Yet, while displaying a strong inclination toward Biel, to the point of committing most of Biel's writings to memory,[11] Luther also exhibits a subtle yet significant independence of thought.

- 2 -

For Biel, the *synteresis* is an inborn possession of human nature which had not been eradicated by the Fall. The *synteresis*, as the point of contact between the human and Divine, is the highest affective power informing the conscience. It affords the self with a predisposed inclination directing human actions toward good. The *synteresis* provides a volitional force as well as a cognitive content -- a desire to do the good as well as a knowledge of the good that is to be done.

Luther as well believed that human nature contains a "residue of former goods"[12] which are "incapable of being obscured."[13] In his *scholia* to Psalm 41, Luther argues that the "*synteresis* and desire (for) good" exist in human nature "*inextinguishably.*"[14] For Luther, as for Biel, the "*synteresis* is a preservation, a remainder or left-over portion of our nature in the corruption and faultiness of perdition. It is like a tinder, a seed, and the material of our future revival and the restoration of our nature."[15]

Luther's position regarding the *synteresis* is significantly similar to that advocated by Gabriel Biel. In many respects, however, both in terms of function and content, it is also surprisingly distinct.

26

For Luther, as for Biel, the *synteresis* is associated with the activities of the conscience. However, whereas for Biel the conscience provides the self with a natural inclination or potency (*potentia*) to do good, for Luther, on the other hand, the *synteresis* is the "witnessing portion" (*superstite portione*)[16] of the conscience. By this Luther means that the *synteresis* is the source of the complaint the conscience makes when the will has chosen to do something other than it should. "(W)hen the soul has sinned, soon the rumbling begins" and it is "the murmur of the *synteresis*" which condemns the self for the sinful choices that have been made.[17] The impious "sense themselves to be accused by conscience and censured by the *synteresis* which ask(s): Why do you do evil?"[18]

These references indicate subtle yet nevertheless significant distinctions between Luther's conception of the *synteresis* and its relationship to the conscience and that of Gabriel Biel. For Biel, the *synteresis* is the agent of good works in that it engenders and inclines the will toward good, whereas for Luther, the will is the agent of all works. The *synteresis*, via the activity of the conscience, judges, condemns and creates pangs of guilt and feelings of remorse within the agent leading to the distress-filled cry for forgiveness on the part of the sinner.

While Luther differed from Biel regarding the function of the *synteresis* and its relationship to the conscience, there was further disagreement regarding the relationship of the *synteresis* to the mind and will of God. This was to prove even more decisive. For both Biel and Luther, the *synteresis* was the remnant of a pre-fallen Adamic purity -- a state of natural conformity with the mind and will of God. It is this conformity which provides the conscience with its basic theological insight and which in turn forms the ontological foundation for the activities of the conscience. However, according to Luther, Biel's belief that one's actions are the direct external manifestation of an inner nature, which is in conformity to the mind and will of God, can effectively still the activity of the conscience. To be more specific, Luther held that the *synteresis* as a source of theological insight is "impeded in many."[19] The function of the *synteresis*, and

27

therefore the conscience, is not infallible but is liable to err, for it is not in perfect conformity to the mind and will of God as Biel believed. In his *De propria sapientia et voluntate* (*On the Proper Wisdom and Will*) Sermon of 1514, Luther writes:

> Just as the *synteresis* of the reason is in conformity with the wisdom of God, it is obvious that the whole reason is by no means in conformity with Him, and so also is the *synteresis* of the will in conformity with the will of God.[20]

Although Luther maintained a twofold *synteresis*, which was similar in many respects to that advocated by Biel, he specifically points to the self's lack of conformity to the mind and will of God. He thereby establishes the limitations of the *synteresis*. While it is obvious that Luther was significantly influenced by Biel, it is also clear that he was dissatisfied with Biel's formulation.

- 3 -

There are several possible influences upon Luther during this period which may be singled out as having led to Luther's dissatisfaction with Biel's formulation of the *synteresis*. The first and most obvious may have been Luther's acceptance of traditional Ockhamist epistemology. During this period, Luther still considered himself, philosophically at least, as an Ockhamist and referred to William of Ockham as "my teacher."[21] It could be argued that Luther was more radically Ockhamist than was Biel and that he may simply have considered the *synteresis* as another of those Platonic meta-categories traditionally rejected by Ockhamist epistemology. Luther's acceptance of the epistemological starting point of Ockhamism, namely that 'essences' and 'universals' are mental constructs rather than necessarily corresponding to or having a reality in and of themselves, may in turn have resulted in an inherent methodological skepticism which prepared him for questioning Biel's reintroduction of the *synteresis*.

Another possible reason for Luther's dissatisfaction with the *synteresis* may be traced to the intense Biblical study and exegesis which Luther was engaged in at this time. Luther was clearly attempting to develop a way of theologizing, grounded firmly in Scripture. Hence, it may be argued that Luther applied Scripture itself as a sort of Ockhamist 'razor,' eliminating from theology all that is not explicitly mentioned in Scripture.

Luther's Biblical study must undoubtedly be acknowledged as extremely significant for a proper understanding of his development. However, one cannot legitimately conclude that Biblical study was in itself the source of his dissatisfaction with the *synteresis*, for it begs the question of the spectacles with which Luther read Scripture. After all, while it must be acknowledged that the *synteresis* does not exist in Scripture *per se*, this is not to say that it is not alluded to. Nor is it to suggest that the theological foundation for a legitimate postulating of the *synteresis* does not exist in Scripture, as held by many generations of theologians from the time of the early Church Fathers.

Furthermore, if we are to accept either of these lines of reasoning, the question that remains unanswered is why Luther continued to believe the "the theological *synteresis*, is in every man and is incapable of being obscured."[22] Given the fact that the *synteresis* is certainly not Ockhamist and unlikely Biblical, why did Luther maintain it at all while obviously critical of it? The key to both aspects of the question points to Luther's growing affinity to the thought of one man -- Saint Augustine (c. 354-430).

B. *Contra* Pelagius

- 1 -

Martin Luther began his career within the devotional and intellectual context of the Augustinian monastery of the Friars Minor of Saint Augustine. As an Augustinian, Luther was generally acquainted with the writings of Augustine, some of which he annotated as early as 1509.[23] It was not until 1515, however, that Luther was to become aware of Augustine's dispute with the fourth century British monk, Pelagius (c. 360-420).[24] It was in this dispute that Luther was to see in bold relief the issues which were to become the basis for his own dispute with Biel and much of late medieval scholasticism.

Pelagius believed that Augustine's predestinarian tendencies had imbued Christianity with a fatalism and determinism. In opposition to Augustine's doctrine of predestination, Pelagius taught that Christians were free to initiate their own salvation. God is necessarily required and obligated to reward that which is morally good with what had been taken away, namely eternal life. Pelagius' first concern was ethical. He affirmed humanity's natural capacity to choose and act, so that there would be no justification for a lack of zeal in pursuit of virtue. But in his attempt to stress freedom of the will and human responsibility, Pelagius tended to minimize the effect of sin on human nature to the point of denying original sin. Pelagius believed that Adam's sin injured himself alone, not the entire human race. This led him to claim in *Pro libero arbitrio* that "everything good and everything evil, in respect of which we are either worthy of praise or blame is done by us, not born with us."[25]

Augustine, in the tradition of Pauline theology, on the other hand, argued that "a man's free choice avails only to lead him to sin."[26] Humanity has the inherited disposition to sin and thus cannot merit redemption or salvation on the basis of its own initiative. Whereas Pelagius affirmed a free will, Augustine placed the emphasis upon the bondage of sin and the need for 'irresistible' grace.

At the same time as his dispute with Pelagius, Augustine was involved on a second front in a dispute with Manichaeaism, a movement of which he himself was a former member. Manichaeaism was more extreme than even Gnosticism in its condemnation of matter as evil in itself. It emphasized the inherent evil of human nature and argued that salvation from the throes of evil can only be accomplished by ascetic means. As an antidote to the radical asceticism advocated by Manichaeaism, Augustine emphasized the role of grace. In opposition to the Manichaean view of human nature as radically evil, Augustine emphasized the significance of the *synteresis*. This again was simply to lead to further charges of determinism by Pelagius.

No doubt Luther maintained the *synteresis* for the same reason as had Augustine, namely as a traditional antidote against Manichaeaism, although in Luther's case it is more likely that he had in mind the Manichaean revival of the twelfth and thirteenth centuries.[27] However, it was Augustine's anti-Pelagian thesis that was of greater significance to Luther, for in it he was to find the key to his own dispute with contemporary theology.

- 2 -

It is unlikely that Augustine's anti-Pelagian thesis would ever have become decisive for Luther had it not been for another significant influence. After all, Biel was certainly aware of the Ockhamist tendency toward Pelagianism and he was careful never to state explicitly that it was possible to attain salvation by one's own efforts without an infusion of grace. Augustine's struggle with Pelagius should therefore have remained an historical footnote were it not for the influence of the former General of Luther's own Order and precursor of a strong

Augustinian tradition at Wittenberg, known after him as the *via Gregorii* --
Gregory of Rimini (d. 1358).

Gregory, the *Doctor authenticus* who established the *schola Augustiniana
moderna*, was generally considered to have been the leading Augustine scholar of
his age.[28] However, Gregory was also an Ockhamist and it was during his time
that Pope John XXII stigmatized three of fifty-one Ockhamist theses as Pelagian.
Feeling obligated to respond to this condemnation, Gregory turned to Augustine
for support.

It is difficult to judge whether Gregory simply used Augustine to justify
certain Ockhamist tenets or whether he actually believed that he had found in
Augustine's writings positions which coincided with those of Ockham.[29] In any
event, in trying to blunt the charges of Pelagianism, Gregory followed
Augustine's lead and argued for the insufficiency of works and the prior necessity
of grace. Gabriel Biel was later to argue against Gregory on precisely this
Pelagian point.

While Biel never suggested that humanity is able to accomplish its own
salvation, he did argue that humanity possesses the natural abilities to be able
to fulfill the command to love God above all else without grace. In fact, Biel
held that by freely choosing to love God above all else, we merit grace which
God 'infallibly' grants as a reward. As Biel writes: "By ... the right attitude
toward God chosen with free will a man can merit ... grace."[30]

Biel's interest in what humanity can do naturally and apart from grace
originates in his concern to show that, by means of the *synteresis*, humanity
possesses the possibility of preparation for the reception of grace -- which
remains as a prerequisite for salvation.[31] A strict charge of Pelagianism would
be entirely accurate only if Biel were to claim that it is possible to earn salvation
solely on the basis of our own efforts without the need for grace, which is clearly
not the case. Nevertheless, it can be argued, as does Luther, that to affirm that
humanity has the natural ability to know and freely choose to do the will of God
as preparation for the reception of grace contains within itself a semi-Pelagianism

in that the self initiates the process and therefore grace as free gift ultimately becomes superfluous.

Had Luther not become aware of the dispute between Gabriel Biel and Gregory of Rimini, Augustine's anti-Pelagian thesis may never have become available to him as a touchstone by which to gauge the validity of contemporary theological propositions.[32] It was Augustine's spectacles that allowed Luther's gaze to become fixed clearly on the issues of sin, grace and works. Luther sided with Gregory, referring to him as "the only scholastic clean on the Pelagian issue."[33] Gabriel Biel was to become the particular focus of Luther's critique. "Gabriel Biel says everything well," writes Luther, "except when he talks about grace, charity, hope, faith, the virtues about which he Pelagianizes as much as his Scotus."[34]

- 3 -

Luther began his lectures on Romans (1515-1516) barely a month after having completed his Psalms lectures. His newfound awareness of Augustine's anti-Pelagian thesis, now given further support by his intensive reading and exegesis of Paul, deepened Luther's dissatisfaction with the way in which the issues of sin, grace and works were dealt with by contemporary theologians.

For Luther, Biel was not taking the radical nature of sin seriously. Biel's stress on the inherent, predisposed inclination toward knowing and doing the good, based on the exaggerated claims of the *synteresis*, required only that sin be avoided and that good works be done in imitation of the example of Christ in preparation for the reception of grace, righteousness and, ultimately, salvation. Luther, on the other hand, argued for the egocentrism of human nature. He considered this so pervasive a condition that it cannot be eliminated by means of the *habitus*, the *facere quod in se est* or any other methodological doctrine espousing a self-initiated *actum meritorium* for which grace and ultimately salvation are 'inevitably' granted as a reward.

We are guilty of sins of which we are not even aware, whether by being unable to recognize the ramifications of actions we believe to be good, or whether by the failure of our reason or intent of our will. We do not know nor can we will what is good for God nor for others.[35] In direct contradistinction to most scholastic anthropology and moral theory, Luther writes:

> It is said that human nature knows and wills good in a general and universal sense, but errs and does not will good in particular cases. It would be better to say (the reverse): human nature ... neither knows nor wills good .... And this harmonizes with Holy Scripture, which describes man as turned in upon himself so that not only corporeal but also spiritual goods are turned to himself, and he seeks himself in all things. Now this curvedness is natural; it is a natural fault and a natural evil. Therefore, he does not receive help from his natural powers, but must seek it from another more powerful help, which is not in himself.[36]

Luther believed that his real opponent was Aristotle. It was not Aristotelian philosophy *per se* to which Luther objected but rather the Pelagianism which he believed was the inevitable consequence of its adoption by Christian theology. Luther writes, "The ancient Fathers ... spoke about these things differently, according to the method of Scripture. But they (scholastics) follow the method of Aristotle in his *Ethics*, and he bases sinfulness and righteousness and likewise the extent of their actualization on what a person does."[37]

It was the absorption of Aristotelian philosophy and anthropology into Christian theology which gave action priority over being and made the exterior life more important than the interior. The belief, that what a person is, is the result of what a person does effectively removes the issues of sin and grace from any discussion of human nature and relegates them solely to the realm of works. This, Luther believes, is the underlying reason why "(o)ur theologians twisted sin so that it applies to works alone."[38] And this is why Luther argues that "the whole of Aristotle's *Ethics* is the worst enemy of grace."[39]

34

- 4 -

Intimately intertwined with the relegation of sin and grace to the realm of works was the issue of the *synteresis*. Ultimately it is impossible to determine whether the establishment of the *synteresis* in fact relegated sin and grace to the realm of works or whether establishing sin and grace in the realm of works necessitated the postulation of the *synteresis*. In either event, the mutual complementariness of these factors provided the basis for scholasticism's emphasis on works and thereby established the foundation for the prevalence of the entire late medieval merit system. Luther's critique of the synergistic nature of the late medieval doctrine of works takes place on these three fronts -- the scholastic understanding of sin, grace and the *synteresis*.

Luther argues that Biel and the scholastics do not really understand the true nature of sin, "(f)or they reduced sin to some very minute activity of the soul" (*motum animi*). In that the self possesses the *synteresis*, "it is inclined albeit weakly, toward the good. And this minute motion toward God (which humanity can perform by nature in co-operation with grace) they imagine to be an act of loving God above all things! But take a good look at man, entirely filled with evil lusts (notwithstanding that minute motion)."[40]

For Luther it is not the natural being who, on the basis of the *synteresis*, is free to initiate righteousness and salvation. Rather, the reverse is true. *Peccatum originale* entails corruption and damnation. "Our weakness lies not in our works but in our nature. Our person, nature, and entire being are corrupted through Adam's fall."[41] We do not disobey the directives of the *synteresis* only in regard to particular works, but our entire life is one of disobedience. Not only *peccatum* but *peccator*.

It is clear that Luther had come to consider an exaggerated view of the efficacy of the *synteresis* to underlie the claim that it is possible to will to love God above all else. Luther outrightly denied this natural ability, arguing that

"Man cannot have such a will from himself, because he is always inclined to evil to such an extent that only through the grace of God is it possible to be moved to good."[42]

It must be emphasized that at this stage of his development Luther was as yet criticizing only the exaggerated claims made for the *synteresis* and not the *synteresis* itself. He continued to maintain it as a central component of his understanding of human nature. In his commentary on the phrase "there is none righteous" in Romans 3:10, the perfect passage for a plausible rejection of the *synteresis* entirely, Luther is still able to write that, "we are not so totally inclined toward evil that there is not a remainder of us which is affected toward the good, as is evident in the *synteresis*."[43] Luther thus staves off the danger of Manichaeaism, as had Augustine. Nevertheless, he is still able to claim that the natural being "is always inclined toward evil" (*semper ad malum inclinatus*).[44] Our will and reason are corrupt for "by nature every man is a sinner"[45] despite the 'minute motion' of the *synteresis*.

- 5 -

In 1517 Luther wrote his famous *Disputatio Contra Scholasticam Theologiam* in which he was to reject specifically many of the basic premises of Gabriel Biel and much of late medieval scholasticism. For Gabriel Biel, the *synteresis* provided a point of contact between God and humanity within the self which in turn provided a natural predisposed inclination toward conformity to correct moral precepts. It was this natural conformity, based entirely on the exaggerated claims of the efficacy of the *synteresis*, that Luther rejected in thesis 6 of his *Disputatio*: "It is false to state that the will can by nature conform to correct precept. This is said in opposition to (John Duns) Scotus and Gabriel (Biel)."[46] Although we may have this *synteresis*, our will is still not inclined toward good, for it has been corrupted by self-interest and pride. Thus in thesis

14 Luther writes: "Nor is it surprising that the will can conform to erroneous and not to correct precept."[47] Rather than emphasizing a conformity of will and reason with the Divine as had Biel, Luther was stressing a deformity. Sin is so pervasive in its effect that (thesis 15): "Indeed it is peculiar to it that it can *only* conform to erroneous and not to correct precept."[48]

Although not explicitly stated, we have with this statement the basis for Luther's later rejection of the *synteresis*. With his assertion that humanity can 'only' conform to erroneous and not to correct precept, Luther has for all intents and purposes rejected the *synteresis* as a natural point of contact between God and humanity which the self is able to actualize on the basis of its own initiative in cooperation with grace.[49] Luther held that to postulate the *synteresis* led to an exaggerated view of human capabilities. The actions arising out of the will are not genuinely good works, for they reveal a love of the self rather than a love of God above all else.

Luther had come to realize that to postulate the *synteresis* was to deny the power of sin over human nature and thus to deny the profound need for grace. In light of the *synteresis*, sin ultimately becomes irrelevant and grace superfluous.

- 6 -

After the period of his *Disputatio Contra Scholasticam Theologiam* of 1517 Luther was to reject any theology which claimed that humanity had the natural ability to initiate or even to cooperate in its own salvation. The ramifications of Luther's radical application of the Augustinian and Pauline understanding of the pervasive effect of sin on human nature and its good works applied not only to Biel but to much of late medieval scholasticism. Luther had come to see himself as a latter-day Augustine defending the faith against modern Pelagian heresies. He felt obligated to criticize what he considered as the

Contra Scholasticam Theologiam

Pelagian tendencies inherent within the intellectual foundation of many of the practices of monastic life and the Church in general. He was exhilarated when he found his message was receiving acceptance and gaining allies in Wittenberg. "Our theology and St. Augustine are going ahead, and reign in our University, and it is God's work," writes Luther.[50]

It is important to note that Luther, by the use of the anti-Pelagian thesis, was effectively increasing the qualitative distinction between God and humanity, creature and Creator. However, while emphasizing our impotence in conforming our will to the will of God by any freely chosen or self-initiated *actum meritorium* Luther still held that (thesis 96): "We must make our will conform in every respect to the will of God."[51]

This apparent discrepancy warrants closer examination.

NOTES

1. See *WA* 9, pp. 29-94; see also Laurence Murphy, "The Prologue of Martin Luther to the *Sentences* of Peter Lombard (1509): The Clash of Philosophy and Theology," *Archiv für Reformationsgeschichte*, 67 (1976), pp. 54-75.

2. Next university rank after *Baccalaureus Biblicus.*

3. Luther was later (1517) to annotate this work along with Biel's *Exposition of the Canon of the Mass.*

4. See Erwin Iserloh, "Theology in the Age of Transition," in *From the High Middle Ages to the Eve of the Reformation*, Vol. IV of the series *Handbook of Church History*, ed. Hubert Jedin and John Dolan (West Germany: Herder and Herder / Burns and Oates Ltd., 1970), p. 600; see also Gilson, *History of Christian Philosophy*, p. 499; and Laurence Murphy, "Martin Luther, the Erfurt Cloister, and Gabriel Biel: The Relation of Philosophy to Theology," *Archiv für Reformationsgeschichte*, 70 (1979), pp. 19-20.

5. See Steven Ozment, "Luther and the Late Middle Ages: The Formation of Reformation Thought," in *Transition and Revolution: Problems and Issues of*

38

European Renaissance and Reformation History, ed. R. M. Kingdon (Minneapolis: Burgess Pub. Co., 1974), pp. 109-129.

6. See Heiko A. Oberman, "Headwaters of the Reformation: *Initia Lutheri -- Initia Reformationis*," in *Luther and the Dawn of the Modern Era; Papers for the Fourth International Congress for Luther Research*, ed. Heiko A. Oberman (Leiden: E. J. Brill, 1974), p. 77.

7. These lectures were completed by April of 1515 and after adding some additional material were ready for publication by the autumn of 1516.

8. See *WA* 6, p. 195; *WA* 6, p. 600. Luther considered himself an Ockhamist as late as 1520. Leif Crane argues for an even later date in *Contra Gabrielem*, pp. 14-15. For Luther and Ockhamism, see Baylor, *Action and Person*, p. 17. For Luther's positive references to Ockham, see Gordon E. Rupp, *The Righteousness of God: Luther Studies* (London: Hodder and Stoughton, 1953), *passim*.

9. According to Melanchton; see Pelikan, *From Luther to Kierkegaard*, p. 6.

10. *WA* 9, p. 28.

11. For an analysis of Luther's twofold *synteresis*, see Steven Ozment, *Homo Spiritualis: A Comparative Study of the Anthropology of Johannes Tauler, Jean Gerson and Martin Luther (1509-16) in the Context of their Theological Thought*, Vol. VI of the series *Studies in Medieval and Reformation Thought*, ed. Heiko A. Oberman (Leiden: E. J. Brill, 1969), p. 111.
Ozment believes that Luther's double *synteresis* of 1514 is an original coming together of late medieval nominalism and realism (fn. pp. 139-140). As has been shown, the credit for this synthesis of the two *viae* must go to Biel rather than to Luther.

12. *WA* 3, p. 603.

13. *WA* 56, p. 177.

14. *WA* 3, p. 238; see also *WA* 56, p. 177.

15. *WA* 1, p. 32.

16. *Ibid.*, p. 36.

17. *WA* 3, p. 617.

18. *WA* 55 II, p. 113.

19. *WA* 3, p. 238.

20. *WA* 1, p. 36; see also *WA* 1, p. 32.
For a discussion of the significance of this Sermon see Baylor, *Action and Person*, pp. 157-206, and Ozment, *Homo Spiritualis*, pp. 139-145.

21. *WA Tr.* II, Nr. 244a; see also *WA Tr.* I, Nr. 193 and 338 for positive references to Ockham.

22. *WA* 56, p. 177.

23. These works included Augustine's *De trinitate* and *De civitate Dei.* See *WA* 9, pp. 2-27.
For an analysis of the influence of Augustine on the young Luther, see Bernard Lohse, "Die Bedeutung Augustins für den jungen Luther," *Kerygma and Dogma*, 11 (1965), pp. 116-135.

24. See Erwin Iserloh, "*Sacramentum et Exemplum*: Ein augustinisches Thema lutherischer Theologie," in *Reformata Reformanda: Festgabe für Hubert Jedin zum 17. Juni 1965*, ed. E. Iserloh and K. Repgen (Münster: Verlag Aschendorff, 1965), I, p. 32.

25. Pelagius, *Pro libero arbitrio*, as reprinted in Henry Bettenson, ed., *Documents of the Christian Church*, 2nd ed. (Great Britain: Oxford University Press, 1967), p. 53.

26. Augustine, *De spiritu et littera*, as reprinted in Bettenson, *op. cit.*, p. 54.

27. This Manichaean revival included the Albingenses and Cathari or Bogomiles. See Steven Runciman, *The Medieval Manichee* (New York: Viking, 1961), *passim*.

28. See Oberman, "Headwaters of the Reformation," p. 82; see also Robert Spieler, "Luther and Gregory of Rimini," *Lutheran Quarterly*, 5 (1953), pp. 155-166; and David Steinmetz, "Luther and the Late Medieval Augustinians: Another Look," *Concordia Theological Monthly*, 44 (1973), pp. 245-260.

29. For an analysis of Gregory's understanding of Augustine, see Damascus Trapp, "Augustinian Theology of the 14th Century," *Augustiniana*, 6 (1956), pp. 152ff.; see also Gilson, *History of Christian Philosophy*, pp. 501-503.

30. Biel, *Collectorium*, Lib. II, dist. 27, quest. 1, concl. 4, as quoted by Hägglund, "Background of Luther's Doctrine of Justification," p. 32.

31. See Crane, *Contra Gabrielem*, p. 214; Oberman, *Harvest of Medieval Theology*, p. 163; and Ozment, *Homo Spiritualis*, pp. 166-167.

32. Leif Crane and David Steinmetz argue that Luther read Augustine first and only later found confirmation of his views in Gregory. Leif Crane, "Gregor von Rimini und Luthers Leipziger Disputation," *Studia Theologica*, 22 (1968), p. 31; and David Steinmetz, *Luther and Staupitz: An Essay on the Intellectual Origins of the Protestant Reformation*, in *Duke Monographs in Medieval and Renaissance Studies*, 4 (Durham, North Carolina: Duke University Press, 1980), p. 17.
Heiko Oberman believes that a strong circumstantial case can be built for the earlier influence of Gregory on Luther. Heiko A. Oberman, *Werden und Wertung der Reformation* (Tübingen: JCB Mohr, 1977), pp. 82-140. Given the fact that Luther was not aware of Augustine's anti-Pelagian writings until 1515, in this area, at least, Oberman's thesis appears the more plausible. Still to be resolved is whether it was Gregory's writings or the influence of a *via Gregorii* tradition which informed Luther's thinking.

33. *WA* 2, p. 394; see also *WA* 2, p. 303. See Spieler, "Luther and Gregory of Rimini," pp. 155-166.

34. *WA Br.* 1, 66, as translated by and quoted in E. Gordon Rupp, *Luther's Progress to the Diet of Worms* (New York: Harper & Row/Torchbook, 1964), p. 46.

35. *Non autem quod Deo et aliis* -- *WA* 56, p. 356.

36. *WA* 56, p. 355. This particular passage also reveals Luther's predisposition to rejecting the *cognitio universalis* epistemology of the *via antiqua* in favour of the *cognitio particularis* of Ockhamism.

37. *Ibid.*, p. 273. Cf. Aristotle, *Ethica Nicomachea*, Bk. I, Ch. 13 1103A-B, (McKeon edition), pp. 330-331. Luther lectured on Aristotle's *Ethics* in 1508 or 1509.

38. *LW* 25, p. 262.

39. *LW* 31, p. 13.

40. *WA* 56, p. 237.

41. *WA* 10 I, pp. 508ff.; see also *WA* 8, p. 104 and *LW* 32, pp. 224ff.

42. *WA* 56, p. 237.

43. *Ibid.*, p. 237.

44. *Ibid.*, p. 233.

45. *Ibid.*, p. 276.

46. *LW* 31, p. 9.

47. *Ibid.*, p. 10.

48. *Ibid.* (italics mine).

49. Steven Ozment (*Homo Spiritualis*, p. 193) argues that Luther limits the efficacy of the *synteresis* "to the sphere of particular and legal righteousness" granting a "potential ethical" significance but making it unavailable as a soteriological resource for the initiation of salvation (p. 197). In other words, the *synteresis* has significance only *coram hominibus* and not *coram Deo*.

50. *WA Br.* I, 99, as translated and quoted in Rupp, *Luther's Progress to the Diet of Worms*, p. 46.

51. *LW* 31, p. 15.

III. *IMITATIO CHRISTUS EXEMPLUM*

A. *Emulatio, Imitatio Operis, Imitatio Mentis*

- 1 -

Gabriel Biel believed that salvation was readily attainable by all Christians in co-operation with grace if they voluntarily chose to perform good works and live a righteous life in imitation of the example of Christ. The *imitatio Christi* held a significant place in Biel's soteriological methodology. Biel was not unique in his understanding of the function of the imitation of Christ. Because of the generally held medieval belief in the interrelatedness of morality and salvation, most traditions also accepted the soteriological significance attached to the practice of the imitation of Christ.

The late medieval focus, particularly that of the monastic communities, was set firmly upon the figure of Christ as the paradigmatic example of the Christian experience. The imitation of Christ was the subject of many of the popular devotional classics of Luther's time,[1] including the famous *Imitation of Christ* by Thomas à Kempis.[2]

In this work, as in many others espousing a Biblically-oriented practical piety, the whole of religious experience was grounded in the imitation of Christ. The telling and retelling of the stories of the life and death of Christ and the martyrdom of the saints of the Christian church served more than a purely devotional purpose. They were not intended solely for edification but also served a didactic function. They were to provide practical moral instructions by crystallizing into concrete images appropriate Christian attitudes and modes of behaviour. Late medieval Christianity sought contemporaneousness with the past, not only by means of the church and the sacraments, but also by the repetition of the past through the imitation of patterns of suffering, humiliation, poverty, celibacy, obedience and love as originally displayed by Christ.

For Gabriel Biel, the life, works and death of Christ reveal the mind and will of God for humanity. To the degree to which Christians actively imitate the example of Christ, to that degree are they in conformity to the mind and will of God. Biel's acceptance of the *synteresis*, however, meant that a part of the self was already conformed to the mind and will of God. The Christian needed only to practise and concretize through good works what was already in one by nature. The work originating with Christ awaits completion by our own *obedientia activa*. By means of the imitation of Christ, Christians participate in righteousness until eventually worthy enough to be granted salvation. The *imitatio Christus exemplum* in Gabriel Biel, as in most medieval traditions, was a significant aspect of the process of salvation itself.

Luther generally agreed with the commonly held belief in the value of the imitation of the example of Christ for the Christian life, arguing that "(w)hatever is written about Christ is written for our learning that we might imitate Him .... (A)ll of Christ's deeds are our instructions ..., therefore the narrating or history of the deeds is always intended for our learning, because this image contains everything."[3] In fact, in his Biblically based campaign against osbcurantism and metaphysical speculation, Luther added that "we should not accept what is written about Christ in a speculative way, but as an example for us."[4]

While Luther acknowledges the significance of the imitation of Christ for the Christian life, his understanding of the *imitatio Christi* differed markedly from that of Gabriel Biel and much of late medieval scholasticism and monasticism. Luther had grown progressively critical of the *synteresis* on the basis of his anti-Pelagian thesis. This in turn meant that a more basic and comprehensive transformation of the self, than he had stressed in thesis 96 of his *Disputatio*, was required in order to attain the *conformitas Dei*. Without the prior postulation of the *synteresis*, good works performed in imitation of Christ could never by themselves be efficacious in attaining the comprehensive conformity Luther sought. Luther's rejection of the inherent righteousness of the *synteresis* and criticism of work-righteousness forced him toward a new understanding of the imitation of Christ.

- 2 -

Luther's critical stance in regard to the *imitatio* motif is best exemplified by his reaction to one particular practice of medieval monasticism, namely the imitation of the saints. The models of a proper *obedientia activa* held before the pious included the lives of saints who lived many miles and years distant. The imitation of these saints as practised by the monks was, according to Luther, both useless and foolish. Luther writes: "People ... who want to imitate the works of the saints and glory in their fathers and forefathers as the monks do today, are extremely foolish because all they accomplish is to ape them."[5] Luther was critical of the *imitatio operis* or the imitation of the works of the saints and martyrs. The imitation of Christ is improper if it is a slavish, legalistic or literal mimicry, or merely the emulative repetition of the works of some other. According to Luther:

> The error lies with those who presumptuously proceed to imitate all these works that were accepted by God, and thus want to be regarded as righteous because they claim to do the same as the saints to whom their works were reckoned unto righteousness. But this means to pervert the example of the saints and not at all to imitate them, for it is an attempt to accomplish a righteousness of works.[6]

Imitatio Christus Exemplum

The goal of the imitation of Christ, as formulated by much of medieval Christendom on the basis of scholastic theology, was to attain a *conformitas Dei*. Luther argued that the imitation of Christ, as it was practised, was little more than a useless repetition, mimicry or 'aping' of patterns of behaviour originally displayed by others. While the *imitatio operis* is useless as a means of attaining righteousness, the very fact that it is practised in order to receive merit and elicit a reward from God is 'to pervert the example of the saints and not at all to imitate them.' In fact, in the *scholia* to his commentary on Romans 13:13, Luther questions whether this self-serving attempt at an *imitatio operis* should even be referred to as *imitatio*, or should instead be referred to simply as *emulatio*:

> The term 'emulation' is a very broad word. To 'emulate' means 'to follow after' or 'to pursue.' And just as the term 'to follow' or 'to pursue' is used in both a good and a bad sense ... also 'to emulate' (*emulor*) can be used in these different ways. And it does not properly mean 'to imitate' (*imitari*) .... (E)mulation embraces the good which is beloved and thereby excludes the sharing of this good .... Thus emulation both loves and hates at the same time ... as for example in I Cor. 10:22; 'Do we emulate the Lord?' that is, are we trying to surpass the Lord or do we know more than He does?[7]

The imitation of Christ must not be understood merely as the repetition of works, especially if done in order to receive merit or to achieve righteousness. This does not conform us to the will of God or make us righteous as are the saints. The works-righteousness, meritoriousness and soteriological significance generally attributed to the *imitatio operis* in fact even prevent a proper *conformitas Dei* for the motivation and intentionality are themselves improper. The improper motivation and intentionality, ironically, can also lead to 'a kind of hatred' of that same individual who is to be the recipient of our good works.

While the *emulatio* and *imitatio operis* are useless and even a perversion of the examples of the saints, Luther did not deny that conformity to the will of God requires the imitation of Christ and the saints. He did, however, add an important qualification. Luther writes: "Fools that they are, they do not look first for their spirit in order to become like them, but unconcerned for the spirit they do the same works they did."[8]

Luther stressed a 'concern for the spirit,' a commonality of motivation and intentionality, an *imitatio mentis*, in order 'to become like them.' The *imitatio mentis* represents the internalization and sharing of the basic morality, perceptions, attitudes and beliefs which animated the saints and is exemplified by their works and deeds. The saints do provide an example we should imitate (*imitatio mentis*). But, we must be careful lest we think that the imitation of their works alone (*imitatio operis*) or our self-serving attempts at imitation (*emulatio*) will 'make us like them.' We must guard against believing that we will become righteous or attain salvation simply by doing good works in imitation of them. Luther writes:

> God does not want such works alone. Rather He wills that they happen with desire and a spontaneous will. And when desire and will are not in them they are dead for God and this is first of all a service that is forced, necessitated and imprisoned, which does not please God.[9]

Luther distinguished between external works and internal attitudes, between repeating outward action and assimilating the interior intentions which motivate them. God demands not only actions but attitudes and intentions, not only works but character, not only an aspect of the self but the entire being. Luther emphasized that it is about the quality of the intention with which Christians ought to be occupied rather than the quality of the works as Biel and the scholastics believed. It is only through this 'concern for the spirit,' as expressed by the *imitatio mentis*, that Christians will ever be able to attain a true and proper *conformitas voluntatis Dei*, righteousness and ultimately salvation.

- 3 -

Luther's criticism of the imitation of Christ as practised by much of late medieval Christendom may be partially attributable to his application of

Imitatio Christus Exemplum

Augustine's anti-Pelagian thesis. It was this which led Luther to criticize what he regarded as exaggerated claims made on behalf of the *synteresis* and the works-righteousness which he saw as the inevitable consequence of the absorption of Aristotelian moral theory into theology. In another sense, Luther's 'concern for the spirit' is directly attributable to his adoption and further elaboration of a particular hermeneutical principle. Luther's distinction between the *imitatio operis* and the *imitatio mentis* may be seen as basically an extension or practical application of the hermeneutical distinction between the *littera* and *spiritus* meaning of Scripture.

Luther uses this principle as a means by which to accentuate the difference between the bare narrative of the Biblical text (i.e., letter) from the deeper meaning of Scripture (i.e., spirit). Luther does not reject the historical meaning of the text which had traditionally provided the basis for literal, allegorical, analogical and tropological exegesis. However, he does recognize the temptation and danger of reference to only the letter for this may obscure the hidden meaning of the text intended by the Holy Spirit.[10] The shadow may be mistaken for substance and the sign for the reality signified.[11]

Luther's use of the differentiation between 'letter' and 'spirit,' while distinctive of his approach, was not unique to him. This hermeneutical principle is attributable to an antecedent exegetical tradition -- a tradition which included Luther's friend and Superior, the Vicar General of the Reformed Congregation of the Eremetical Order of Saint Augustine in Saxony and Dean of the theological faculty at Wittenberg -- Johannes von Staupitz (c. 1460-1525).[12]

- 4 -

Von Staupitz did more than provide Luther with the hermeneutical distinction between 'letter' and 'spirit.'[13] Von Staupitz not only contributed to

Luther's methodological principles but he provided some of the content and much of the direction for Luther's later works as well.[14]

Whereas Biel and much of late medieval scholasticism looked to the life of Christ for examples of good works to be imitated by the faithful, von Staupitz pointed to the *passio Christi*. He writes:

> On the hill of Calvary He has shown us a model (*vorbilde*) of all sanctity .... He is a model given by God, according to which I would work, suffer and die. He is the only model which man can follow, in which every good in life, suffering and death is usefully modeled. Therefore, no one can do right, suffer correctly, or die rightly, unless it happens in conformity (*gleichformig*) with the life, suffering and death of Christ.[15]

Von Staupitz endeavoured to show that a Christian must, in all humility, voluntarily bear the cross and endure suffering as Christ voluntarily suffered and bore the cross.

As distinct from much of the monastic devotional meditative tradition, von Staupitz did not believe it was enough to immerse oneself only meditatively in the passion of Christ. The cross must be seen as more than a past event or an allegorical symbol. It must be seen as the centre of the Christian life as it was the central event in the life of Christ. In his work, *Ein Buchlein von der nachfolgung des willigen sterbens Christi* (1515), which Luther heartily endorsed,[16] von Staupitz's motto was *dem nackenden, dem blossen Jesu nackendt und bloss nachfolgen.*[17] Christians must experientially participate in the cross of Christ and this is possible only if one is truly humble as was Christ.

While Biel pointed to the example of the life of Christ, von Staupitz pointed to the cross of Christ; while Biel emphasized performing good works in imitation of Christ, von Staupitz emphasized the humility of Christ. This difference in emphasis and perspective exhibited by von Staupitz is traceable to the influence of Bernard of Clairvaux (1090-1153) and the tradition of affective mysticism.[18]

B. *Humilitas, Resignatio Voluntatis, Descensus ad Infernum*

- 1 -

Mystical thought and terminology were to be found in the most abstruse philosophical treatise as well as in literature intended for the edification of the unschooled Christian. Mystical theology bridged all social classes and religious persuasions. This impregnation of mysticism into the variegated fabric of medieval thought makes it extremely difficult to speak of clearly defined 'schools' of mysticism. However, as was the situation in scholasticism, mysticism must not be viewed as a monolithic movement. While it is difficult to delineate adequately the diverse branches of the mystical tradition, a characteristic point of differentiation among them revolves around their respective approaches to the question of human nature.

Most medieval traditions, including mysticism, pointed to a basic *substantia* underlying human nature, variously referred to either as a soul, *Seelengrund* or *synteresis*. Regardless of the terminology used, in most cases the term represented the sharing of a basic commonality of being with the Divine. Sin was seen as having distorted this natural unity with God; but by means of human effort and the grace of God, Christians are enabled to return to this essential state.

In the tradition of mystical theology generally referred to as Dionysian, the emphasis was placed upon the mind and the belief that the Divine was intellectually knowable. In the affective mystical tradition, as represented by Bernard of Clairvaux, on the other hand, the emphasis was not on the mind or on the scrutiny of divine truth. Rather, the emphasis was placed upon the heart. Love (*caritas*) was the basic principle of 'likeness' with the Divine. It provided the glue bonding creature and Creator.

50

For Bernard, love was not simply a relational term. It also provided a methodology which had as its objective a mystical love-union with the Divine (*unio mystica*) "in which the perfect correspondence of will make of two, one spirit."[19] The image of God is restored in the soul only through the purification of our selves through love. Love is the basis of volitional conformity; it cleanses and allows union to occur. Bernard writes:

> Such conformity unites the soul to the Word. Already resembling Him by nature, it begins to do so by will. It loves as it is loved. If it loves God perfectly then it is wed to Him. What more sweet than this conformity?[20]

Bernard argued that the love of God can only be shown through our imitation of God incarnate.[21] God became imitable in Jesus -- that is, God's love for humanity was revealed in the life, works and death of Jesus Christ. In the historical Jesus, Bernard saw how concupiscence can become charity and how carnal love can become spiritual love. By imitating Christ we as well can attain the deep love for God and humanity which characterized the life of Christ.

Bernard also argued that because the first and, therefore, greatest of sins was pride, the first virtue must be humility. The lack of humility prevents a proper growth and increase of Christian love, for only the humble know themselves for what they truly are, namely, alienated from God, from others and from themselves. Only to the humble is the truth of their own misery revealed. From this realization, charity follows, for in recognizing our own misery, we sympathize with that of our neighbour.[22] The perfection of love is causally dependent on the increase of humility. Humility is essential for a proper love relationship with the Divine. It is necessary, writes Bernard, "for him who wishes to ascend to the lofty mysteries of Divine Love, that he must have a low opinion of himself."[23]

51

- 2 -

Due in part to the considerable influence of Bernard, humility was to become one of the primary virtues of many of medieval traditions. Luther found in mystical theology a history of dissent forming a tradition against tradition. However, while mysticism provided an alternative to scholasticism, this is not to suggest that mysticism and scholasticism were mutually exclusive. It was possible in some senses to be both a scholastic and a mystic. This is particularly true of the Bernardian mystical tradition and nominalism. In fact, these two traditions may even be considered as complementary. The focus on the heart in the Bernardian mystical tradition and the will in nominalism made them natural allies in their criticism of 'speculative' mysticism of the Dionysian variety and the 'speculative' scholasticism of the *via antiqua*, both of which were accused of lacking humility.[24]

Luther acknowledges his relationship to, and in many cases dependence upon, mystical authors by specific approval or disapproval written into the margins of their writings or by explicit references to them in his own writings. Luther often speaks of Dionysius approvingly, particularly in his *Dictata super Psalterium* (1513-1515).[25] However, he also writes, "(I)n his theology, which is rightly called mystical, of which certain ignorant theologians make so much he is downright dangerous, for his is more of a Platonist than a Christian."[26]

Luther was also critical of Bernard, particularly in his understanding of human nature and Bernard's belief that it is possible to attain perfected love. However, he did agree with the significance for the Christian life that Bernard attributed to humility. Luther advocated diligently following Bernard's twelve prescribed steps to humility as outlined in his *Tractatus de gradibus humilitas et superbiae*.[27] Commenting on I Peter 5:5, Luther argues that, "it is to the humble that God gives His grace."[28] Luther accepted the *humilitas* theology to the extent that he could write in his Psalms lectures that "humility alone saves."[29]

- 3 -

Luther had become generally familiar with *humilitas* theology both through his reading of Bernard and through the writings of Johannes von Staupitz. However, the most significant contemporary advocate of a *humilitas* theology who was to exert the greatest influence on Luther's thought was the Parisian theologian, Jacques Lefèvre d'Étaples (c. 1455-1536), better known in Germany by his Latinized name as Jacobus Faber Stapulensis.

Stapulensis was both a nominalist and a mystic. While Gabriel Biel may also be considered a nominalist and a mystic, it would be more accurate to characterize Biel as a nominalist with strong mystical elements.[30] Conversely, it would be more accurate to characterize Stapulensis as a mystic with strong nominalist elements in the tradition of the famous former Chancellor of the University of Paris, Jean Gerson (1363-1429).[31]

Stapulensis was also a Biblical scholar who had come under the considerable influence of Erasmian humanism. He had written several exegetical commentaries, one of which, his *Psalterium Quincuplex* (1509), Luther annotated in 1513 and used in the course of his own lectures on Psalms. In 1512 Stapulensis published his *Epistolae Divi Pauli Apostoli* which Luther used quite extensively for the first eight chapters of his own lectures on Paul's *Epistle to the Romans*.[32]

Stapulensis' exegesis of Scripture was dominated by Christological concerns. His purpose was to reveal the paradigmatic figure of Christ, which he held was hidden throughout Scripture, in even the most unlikely places. He attempted to delineate fully the form of Christ for the purposes of devotion and imitation. Stapulensis realized that the Gospels gave some information. However, gaping omissions remained for those who sought a conception of the life of Christ which would be applicable to all stages and experiences of the Christian life.

Stapulensis rejected the prevalent literal/historical method of exegesis which he considered to be 'the letter which kills.' The literal sense of Scripture "makes David a historian rather than a prophet."[33] Stapulensis was also critical of the allegorical, tropological and analogical methods. These were the typical medieval solutions to the problem of literalism. They enabled the reader to move beyond the narrow confines of the letter in order to derive generalizations and principles from the fragmentary record which could be applied to the many situations faced by contemporary Christians.

Stapulensis claimed he did not want to deny these methods "especially where the content of the text demands it."[34] However, he was unsatisfied with the methods, believing that they were, for the most part, the invention of a self-serving humanity. As such, they could not provide true knowledge of the hidden or 'spiritual' intention of God.

It is at this point that Stapulensis' roots in mystical theology come to the fore. In order to understand the 'spiritual' meaning of Scripture, Stapulensis believed that it was necessary for the reader to be "animated by the Spirit" -- the same spirit which speaks through the prophets and Apostles.[35] This spiritual sense of Scripture is only revealed to those who realize that ignorance is superior to knowledge.[36] In order to prevent the perversion of Scripture by intellectual pride, it is necessary to approach the Word of God with true humility: "Those who approach in presumption and pride are rejected, not just by Paul ... but by Him who resists the proud and gives grace to the humble."[37] It is this spirit of humility which permeates the lives of the prophets, apostles, saints and martyrs of the Christian faith.

Unlike other medieval theologians, Stapulensis did not believe that it was possible to attain the degree of humility required of Christians simply by means of imitating specific works recorded in Scripture or by emulating the works of other Christians.[38] True humility is only attainable through suffering. In this regard, Stapulensis pointed to one characteristic example of the life of Christ which, according to him, stood out beyond all the others and most clearly revealed the hidden will of God for humanity. At its basis the life of Christ is characterized by his descent into hell. According to Stapulensis, to undergo humbly the experience of the *descensus ad infernum* (*infernos*) in imitation of the paradigmatic event was the will of God for humanity.[39]

- 4 -

As a nominalist and mystic, Stapulensis' focus of concern was on the heart and will. It is by means of the suffering and humiliation of the *descensus ad infernum* that Christians are cleansed and purged and then resurrected and justified in imitation of the paradigmatic event. By means of the descent into hell, one is brought to the depths of despair, the lowest levels of existence, to hell and back, as was the primary exemplar, Jesus Christ. The Christian is justified to the degree or depth that the *descensus* is experienced, and the *descensus* is experienced to the degree that one has the humble faith to permit the process of purgation to occur.

This faith stance in regard to the process of *descensus* is referred to by Stapulensis as the *resignatio voluntatis*. It is understood as resigning one's will to the will of God, or of having the naked faith (*nuda fides*) to offer one's life to God who would mold it through suffering, humiliation and despair until self-will is stripped away, pride destroyed, and the will of God put in its place.[40] The continuing process of *resignatio voluntatis* and the *descensus ad infernum* truly imitates the paradigmatic form of the faithful, suffering and humiliated Christ. Through this process the Christian becomes ever more righteous and Christ-like (*similitudo*) until eventually worthy enough to be granted salvation.

55

- 5 -

The differences and similarities between Biel and Stapulensis regarding their respective approaches toward the imitation of Christ are now quite apparent. These are, furthermore, characteristically representative of the two primary attitudes by which the imitation of Christ was approached by late medieval theology. For Gabriel Biel, the *conformitas voluntatis et rationis Dei* consisted of voluntarily performing specific prescribed meritorious works in imitation of Christ for which grace and ultimately salvation are granted. For Stapulensis, conformity to the will of God, righteousness and salvation are also attained by means of the *imitatio Christi*. However, unlike Biel, it was not specific works that were to be imitated (*imitatio operis*). Rather, it was the mind and spirit of the paradigmatic image of the faithful, suffering and humiliated figure of Christ, as revealed throughout Scripture, that was to be imitated (*imitatio mentis*).

Furthermore, while Biel stressed an active obedience to the will of God (*obedientia activa*) on the basis of the inherent capabilities provided by the *synteresis*, Stapulensis as a mystic emphasized a passive stance in relation to the will of God (*obedientia passiva*). The Christian is to be humbly resigned to the suffering and humiliation of the *descensus ad infernum*, for this is God's will for us. It is the *resignatio voluntatis* and the *descensus ad infernum* which truly imitate Christ and are in conformity to the will of God.

C.   Luther and Stapulensis

- 1 -

From Paul and Augustine Luther had learned of the radical corruption of human nature as a result of sin. This in turn led to his rejection of the scholastic belief in the inherent righteousness of human nature (*synteresis*) which could be actualized simply by performing good works in imitation of Christ and the saints and martyrs of the Christian Church.   True righteousness, for one who is *peccator*, is vastly more difficult to attain than learning to master the playing of a musical instrument on the basis of an inborn aptitude.   The active and prescriptive *imitatio operis* of Biel and scholasticism, associated as it was with works-righteousness, meritoriousness and self-justification, denied the true nature of the self. It was in fact a form of spiritual and intellectual pride which is not in conformity to the will of God.

From Stapulensis[41] and Bernard before him, Luther learned that what is required of Christians is not the *obedientia activa*, as advocated by Biel, with its presumptive claim to know and be capable of doing the will of God.   What is required of Christians is a passive stance in relation to the will of God -- the *obedientia passiva*.   Luther writes:

> Only when our own plans have ceased and our works have stopped,
> and we are purely passive in relation to God, both inwardly and in
> our outward activity, are we capable (of receiving) His works and
> plans.[42]

Luther also learned from Stapulensis that the spirit of humility required of Christians can only be attained by resigning oneself to the *descensus ad infernum*.   We must suffer, die and descend into hell as Christ "suffered, died and descended into hell."[43]   Christ who alone was in conformity to the will of God was given to sinful humanity as an example.   Luther points out that even the saints "are killed and descend with (Christ) to hell." In the same sense, "they are resurrected with him and ascend into heaven."[44]

Christians must also be humiliated, suffer and descend into hell in order to die to sin. "We cannot go to heaven," writes Luther, "unless we first go to hell."[45] We must not try to avoid the purgation required of us but must humbly resign ourselves to accepting the *descensus* as the will of God, as did Christ: "In his commentary on Psalm 70, Luther writes: In the same measure as one is humiliated, one is exalted to the highest because of the descent into the ultimate depths first. And this imitates Christ in a proper sense."[46] Resigning oneself to the mortification, suffering and humiliation of the *descensus* 'imitates Christ in a proper sense' (*imitatio mentis*) and is in conformity to the will of God.[47] This is the *via* God has ordained for all humanity: "The way is hard and narrow, to forsake all visible things, to be stripped of all senses, to be led out of all accustomed things, indeed, that is what it means to die and descend into hell."[48]

- 2 -

Primarily due to the influence of Faber Stapulensis and the tradition of Bernardian *humilitas* theology, Luther came to accept the *resignatio voluntatis* and *descensus ad infernum* of the *obedientia passiva* tradition as the way God had established for a sinful humanity. Humbly resigning ourselves to suffering imitates Christ 'in a proper sense' and is in conformity to the will of God.

While generally appearing to side with Stapulensis on the significance of the *resignatio* and *descensus* motifs, Luther could not accept some of the basic presuppositions nor practices of affective mysticism. Luther was now to take the same principles derived from Augustine's anti-Pelagian thesis, which he had used so effectively against Biel and scholasticism, and apply them to Stapulensis and *humilitas* theology.

Within the soteriological context of penitential theology, suffering, humiliation and self-mortification were understood as necessary aspects of the process of purgation. As such, suffering was considered to be a transient condition which was to be willingly and stoically endured, but ultimately transcended. The successful endurance of suffering, whether self-imposed or not, meant the alleviation of suffering. Grace was granted as an aid and as a reward for the successful endurance of voluntary purgation.

Furthermore, although Biel and Stapulensis had respectively different conceptions of the function of the imitation of Christ as the means by which Christians are conformed to the will of God, there was an acceptance by both of the *synteresis* as a point of natural conformity between the human and Divine (although, to be entirely accurate, this belief in the natural conformity to the *synteresis* was not as exaggerated in Stapulensis as it was in Biel). Both also believed that this natural conformity of the *synteresis* could be and needed to be increased in co-operation with the grace of God (although, again to be precise, Stapulensis assigned a greater role to grace than did Biel). Nevertheless, whether the means advocated were those of an *obedientia activa*, as in Biel, or an *obedientia passiva*, as in Stapulensis, both maintained that Christians are capable of attaining righteousness in co-operation with grace, and ultimately salvation for one who was deserving.

Luther had come to accept that it is through resigning ourselves to the suffering mortification of the *descensus ad infernum* that we are conformed to the will of God. But he also came to see that salvation cannot be initiated by a sinful humanity. Suffering, if initiated by the self, is not true suffering. The *resignatio*, as well, cannot be considered as true resignation if the suffering which is to be endured is transient, self-chosen or self-initiated. This does not imitate Christ in a proper sense and thus it is not in conformity to the will of God. To hold that the self can voluntarily initiate the process of salvation denies the very *humilitas* which is required for salvation.

Imitatio Christus Exemplum

Luther argued that a self-chosen or self-imposed imitation of the suffering *Christus exemplum* was simply another form of works-righteousness. It was ultimately no different from imitating the works of Christ. In both cases it was a self-initiated attempt to attain salvation on the basis of a claim to self-justification. In both cases it amounted to a denial of our true status as *peccator* and thus a denial of the profound need for grace. Sin is a real and permanent feature of the human condition. The suffering and despair of the *descensus ad infernum* must therefore also be the experience of a real hell and not the imagined hell of a prescribed spiritual exercise such as fasting, with its implications of merit. The self-serving nature of the exercise denies the very *humilitas* which is required. The imitation of the suffering, humiliated Christ by prescribed ascetic means, as advocated by the penitential mystical tradition, was simply another form of *actum meritorium*. It did not represent a true bearing of the cross. Although one can lose weight by fasting or starvation, they must be regarded as qualitatively different, simply because one is self-chosen and control is maintained by the initiator.

Luther continued to advocate the *resignatio voluntatis* and the *descensus ad infernum* as representing a proper imitation of Christ, as had Stapulensis. But, as a consequence of his radical analysis of the depth of the effect of sin on human nature and the resulting profound need for grace, he added an important qualification -- we cannot carry a cross of our own choosing. Rather we must resign ourselves to bearing the cross thrust upon our backs. Only resigning ourselves to true suffering imitates Christ in a proper sense and is in conformity to the will of God. Indeed Christ did not seek the cross, "No, He waited until it was God's will that He should drink the cup. He should be the model for us to imitate."[49]

Although Stapulensis had helped to place Luther's feet on the path toward the reformation with his emphasis upon the suffering, humiliated Christ, the *resignatio voluntatis*, the *descensus ad infernum* and the *obedientia passiva*, he had not taken Luther far enough. Suffering conforms us to the will of God, but *conformitas* cannot be achieved on the basis of human effort. Conformity to the will of God as a requirement of salvation must itself be understood entirely as the prerogative of God.

- 3 -

The *synteresis* and the *actum meritorium*, evident in both Biel and Stapulensis, had become understood by Luther as sheer metaphysical speculation. They amounted to attempts to choose our own means of salvation and achieve that goal on the basis of our own efforts. They represent an intellectual pride or 'wisdom of the flesh' derived from "blind reason and heathen ways of thinking."[50] Luther writes:

> (T)he wisdom of the flesh dissipated the conformity of the will with God, so that it does not wish for what it ought to, and that for which the will of God wishes in order to save it. Rather the will seems in itself to be happy and to be saved by that which the man himself chooses. For discord arises between God and man here, it is apparent, in the means and not the ends.[51]

Both God and humanity desire the same 'end' for humanity (i.e., salvation) but humanity is not willing to accept the 'means' or way chosen by God. Not only are the means of salvation chosen by medieval theology not in conformity to the will of God but they are in fact antithetical.

The way of salvation offered by God "is a way clear contrary to our notions."[52] True righteousness and salvation require the exact opposite of that advocated by medieval theology. "We ask to be saved and He in order that He may save us first damns."[53] The rejection of this damnation is thus paradoxically also the rejection of salvation, for in the attempt to preserve our will we in fact reject the will of God. "The damned are tortured because they are not willing to be damned, nor resign themselves to this will of God."[54]

Only if we humbly accept our true status *coram Deo* as *peccator* do we see with our own eyes who we are in God's sight. Only if we condemn and accuse ourselves (*condemnatio sui, accusatio sui*) does our judgment agree with God's judgment, and only then are we in conformity to the will of God:

> He who justifies himself, condemns God .... He who judges himself and confesses his sin ... has said about himself that which God has said about him. And thus he now conforms to God and is true and righteous, for so is God with whom he agrees.[55]

Those who in true humility acknowledge and confess basic sinfulness and the inability to earn or merit salvation on the basis of good works or an inherent 'goodness' have conformed their judgment to the judgment of God. The humble acceptance of God's strict and condemning judgment of the self as sinner is in conformity to the will of God. This same conformity in turn becomes the reason one is not condemned by God.

The unacknowledged and unconfessed sinner, in attempting to define what is sin and what is salvation, sins doubly (*duplex peccatum*). The acknowledged and confessed sinner, by the very admission of being a sinner, is paradoxically not a sinner, for by 'becoming' a sinner one also becomes righteous. "Be a sinner to yourself and you will be righteous before God."[56]

An intrinsic negative self-judgment is in conformity to the will of God. It becomes in turn the basis for a positive extrinsic judgment and the forgiveness of a merciful and loving God.

D.　*Opus Alienum Dei, Opus Proprium Dei, Sola Gratia*

- 1 -

Luther argued that God "condemns what men choose and chooses what men condemn. And this judgment has been shown us in the cross of Christ."[57] The way of salvation is a *via contrarii* -- a way of suffering, humiliation, damnation, resignation and descent into hell. This soteriological understanding is paralleled by one of the most persistent and distinctive theological themes Luther deals with -- namely, the hiddenness of God. The revelation of God is hidden under the form of contrary appearance (*Deus absconditus sub contrario*).[58]

The God revealed in Scripture is a God who works contrary to human expectations. What is apparent in the life and death of Christ is weakness not strength,[59] folly not wisdom,[60] humiliation not victory.[61] The power and glory of God are hidden "in the humility and shame of the cross."[62] The underlying reality is not visible, and is in fact in contrast to, ordinary expectations.[63]

The *Deus absconditus sub contrario* and the subsequent *via contrarii* of salvation, with its emphasis on *humilitas* and the *descensus ad infernum*, are all aspects of a general theological motif that Luther was later to refer to as a *theologia crucis*.[64] Luther's theology of the cross, although distinctive of his early career, was not unique to him. Luther shared with penitential mysticism many of the same themes which together comprise his theology of the cross.[65] With Bernard, von Staupitz and Stapulensis, Luther advocated that conformity to the will of God requires an *obedientia passiva* and entails purgation and suffering. Where Luther differs with the theology of the cross of penitential mysticism is more a matter of degree than of theological substance.

Luther believed that conformity to the will of God requires suffering. But he had also come to believe that salvation is not attainable by a sinful humanity on the basis of human efforts, initiatives or merits. Even suffering cannot be self-imposed in order to attain merit. In his *glosses* to Romans 8:29 Luther argues that the motivation involved in the self-initiated suffering of a prescribed spiritual or ascetic exercise is self-serving and thus denies and perverts the very end which is sought. In contrast to most medieval theology, Luther rejected any and all soteriological resources in human nature or actions. They cannot "become such people by their merit, for then (Paul) would have said ... people who would conform themselves."[66] Both the means and conditions for salvation must be seen entirely as the free gift of God.

63

- 2 -

Luther had established that conformity to the will of God is the precondition for salvation. He also argued that conformity to the will of God entails humbly resigning oneself to suffering. Death is overcome not by power or strength but by infirmity, weakness and suffering. Christ teaches us by his example that we must confidently endure suffering and death. This is the will of God for humanity as revealed in the cross of Christ. However, Luther had also come to believe that suffering cannot be self-imposed, self-initiated or self-chosen. Whereas Luther previously argued that salvation is the gift of God, he now includes the way of salvation as the gift of God as well. It is God who "leads down to hell and brings back."[67] Suffering is paradoxically a sign of God's grace.

Luther takes up the theme of God's work of grace and develops it in his St. Thomas' Day sermon of December 21, 1516. Referring to Isaiah 28:21, Luther argues that it is by means of the trials (*Anfechtungen*), tribulations, vicissitudes and uncertainties (*tribulatio, tentatio, compunctio*) of daily existence that God "reveals to us that we are sinners, unrighteous, liars, miserable, foolish and lost."[68] It is these trials which destroy our presumption and prevent pride from arising. Luther further argues that because "God can make just only those who are not just, He is compelled to perform an alien work in order to make them (conscious of being) sinners, before He performs His proper work of justification."[69]

Luther refers to the first part of the damnation/justification equation as the 'strange' (Isaiah 28:21) or 'bitter' (Rev. 10:9-10) work of God -- the *opus alienum Dei*, while referring to the second part of the equation as the 'sweet' (Rev. 10:9-10) or 'proper' work of God -- the *opus proprium Dei*.[70] In his sermon Luther develops the motif of the *opus alienum et proprium Dei* further:

> God's alien work ... is the suffering of Christ and sufferings in
> Christ, the crucifixion of the old man and the mortification of

Adam. God's proper work however is the resurrection of Christ, justification in the Spirit, and the vivification of the new man, as Romans 4 (.25) says: Christ died for our sins and was raised for our justification. Thus conformity with the image of the Son of God includes both of these works.[71]

There are several nuances in the preceding reference indicating significant shifts in Luther's thought on a variety of fronts. While Luther continues to stress suffering as the basis for *conformitas*, there is a greater emphasis upon 'conformity with the image of the Son of God' rather than on a *conformitas voluntatis Dei*. The most obvious shift, however, is Luther's uniting of suffering and grace within his understanding of the *opus suum Dei*.

- 3 -

Luther believed that "We must suffer so that we may be conformed to Christ."[72] Furthermore "it is inevitable that you will have to become conformable to Christ's image and suffering."[73] Conformity to the image of the suffering and humiliated Christ is seen by Luther as the precondition for the reception of God's proper work of justification and vivification.[74] Luther was prepared to refer to this suffering as the *kakangelion*, the 'bad news' in contrast to the 'good news' of salvation.[75] Mortification and suffering are integrally related to God's grace. "Who knows," writes Luther, "whether with the removal of suffering God's grace may also be taken from us."[76]

It is not the case that there are two Gods: a loving God and a wrathful God. Nor is it the case that the two expressions of God's wrath and love are in conflict with each other. If this were the case, the Ockhamist God of pure arbitrariness and capriciousness, the *Deus exlex* bound by no law, to which Luther had always objected, would be reintroduced. God's true nature is love, and wrath is alien to that nature. But wrath is the means which God has chosen to help a sinful humanity fight against its own sinfulness. "Wrath is truly God's alien work, which He employs contrary to His nature because He is forced into it by the wickedness of man."[77]

The ability to stand up under the bitter wrath of the alien work of God by which we are conformed to the suffering, humiliated Christ must not be understood as based upon the power, strength or ability of the self to stoically endure suffering.   This belief, characteristic of the tradition of penitential mysticism, again displays a lack of genuine humility.   Rather, as Luther maintains, at the moment of despair 'those unutterable groanings begin' and the Spirit helps our infirmities: "(W)ithout the help of the Spirit, it would be impossible for us to stand up under this activity of God, in which He hears and fulfills what we pray for."[78]

God's wrath is most terrible when the sinner is not punished but allowed to remain sinful.

> When God speaks, shows His wrath, is angry, punishes, gives us into the hands of our enemies, sends plagues, hunger, the sword and other troubles, it is a certain sign that He is gracious to us. If however, He says 'I will no longer punish you but be silent, withdraw my wrath from you, and let you go on and do whatever you want as you think best,' this is a sign that he has turned away from us. But the world and our reason turn this upside down and think that the opposite is true.[79]

It is due to our *insapientia* that the alien work of God as subjectively experienced appears to be the work of a wrathful God and is often unrecognizable as an expression of divine grace that has its source in a loving God.   Both the *opus alienum Dei* and the *opus proprium Dei*, by which we are conformed to Christ, must be seen to work together as expressions of the love and grace of God. Beyond the subjective perception of the paradoxical dyadic will of God, which both damns and justifies, lies a loving and transcendent God with a salvific will for humanity.

In light of this theological perception, Luther argues that grace must not be understood as a once and for all static possession, a possession which endows the soul with a righteousness that the person is then merely obliged to actualize. Neither is grace a reward for the successful endurance of suffering which infuses the self with a new spiritual quality. Rather, suffering as a sign of God's condemnation of the sinner is itself the gift of a loving God granting us the very conformity we long for. Grace, as revealed in the cross of Christ, is a dynamic process. It is that event or series of events which allows us to see ourselves as we really are in relation to God, making it possible to recognize the true nature of sin, revealing our strengths as weaknesses and our righteousness as unrighteousness.

We are conformed to Christ by both the alien and proper work of God. The alien work of God (which we tend to resist) and the proper work of God (which we tend to welcome) do for us what we cannot do for ourselves. However, it is not the case that we must first undergo damnation to rid us of sin, thereafter becoming progressively more righteous. Damnation and righteousness, suffering and redemption, death and resurrection are not successive moments in the Christian life -- they are two sides of the single reality of grace and occur with some simultaneity. Both are expressions of God's unmerited grace and love. The alien work of God in conforming us to the image of Christ is the gift of a loving God in the creative process of fulfilling our prayers. The crucifixion of the sinner is as much a gift of God as is the new life in Christ. Conformity to the image of the Son of God, which is necessary for salvation, is granted to us by grace alone. *Sola gratia* had become Luther's central theological dictum for a sinful humanity.

- 4 -

While moving forward in his undertaking to establish *sola gratia* as the central and sole facet of soteriological reality, Luther was simultaneously altering his understanding of *conformitas*. While originally accepting Biel's understanding of *conformitas voluntatis et rationis Dei*, the influence of nominalism, together with that of affective penitential mysticism, had led Luther to place a greater emphasis on the will and *conformitas voluntatis Dei*. The influence of Scripture and Stapulensis in turn resulted in an increased conviction that the will of God for humanity is fully revealed in the paradigmatic form of the suffering and humiliated Christ. One should not be overly concerned with the hidden God but "should be satisfied with what is revealed."[80] Slowly but surely Luther was moving away from his theocentric understanding of *conformitas voluntatis Dei* to an understanding of "conformity with the image of the Son of God."[81] The development of this new Christological orientation merits further clarification.

NOTES

1. For an analysis of the *imitatio Christi* in monastic devotional literature and practise of the late medieval period, see Darrell Reinke, "Martin Luther: Language and Devotional Consciousness," *The Spirituality of Western Christendom*, in *Cistercian Studies Series* No. 30: *Studies in Medieval Culture*, ed. E. R. Elder (Michigan: Cistercian Publications Inc., 1976), pp. 152-168.

2. There are no references to suggest that Luther was influenced by this particular work. However it was readily available to Luther and it would be surprising if he were not familiar with it.

3. *WA* 56, p. 137.

4. *Ibid.*

5. *LW* 25, p. 195.

6. *Ibid.*, pp. 263-264.

7. *Ibid.*, pp. 483-484.

8. *Ibid.*, pp. 195.

9. *WA* 7, p. 300.

10. *WA* 55 I, p. 2.

11. *WA* 3, p. 318.

12. The Augustinian Eremites were a mendicant order incorporated by Innocent IV in 1243. By 1450 they comprised almost 2000 Chapters. See Rupp, *Luther's Progress to the Diet of Worms*, p. 15.

13. See David Steinmetz, "Hermeneutic and Old Testament Interpretation in Staupitz and the Young Martin Luther," *Archiv für Reformationsgeschichte*, 70 (1979), pp. 24-58. Cf. D. R. Reinke, "From Allegory to Metaphor: More Notes on Luther's Hermeneutical Shift," *Harvard Theological Review*, 66 (1973), pp. 386-395.

14. Luther was later (1533) to claim, "Staupicus hat die doctrinam angefangen" (*WA Tr.* 2, Nr. 526). David Steinmetz in his study, *Luther and Staupitz*, shows that this statement was essentially another one of Luther's many unrestrained exaggerations.

15. I. Knaake, ed., *Johannis Staupitii Opera*, I (Potsdam, 1867), p. 62, as quoted in Reinke, "Martin Luther: Language and Devotional Consciousness," p. 158.
     For an analysis of the *imitatio Christi* in von Staupitz, see Ernst Wolf, "Johannes von Staupitz und die theologischen Anfange Luthers," *Luther Jahrbuch*, (1929), pp. 56ff.

16. *WA Br.* 1, 381.

17. As quoted in Steinmetz, *Luther and Staupitz*, p. 77.

18. See David Steinmetz, *Misericordia Dei: The Theology of Johannes von Staupitz in its Late Medieval Setting*, Vol. IV of the series *Studies in Medieval and Reformation Thought* (Leiden: E. J. Brill, 1968); also John J. Staudt, "John Staupitz on God's Gracious Love," *Lutheran Quarterly*, 8 (1956), pp. 225-244.

19. Bernard, *Sermons* LXXXIII.3.

20. *Ibid.*

21. See J. Leclerq, "The Imitation of Christ and the Sacraments in the Teaching of St. Bernard," *Cistercian Studies*, 9 (1974), *passim*. For an analysis of Luther's place in this tradition see K.-H. zur Mühlen, *Nos Extra Nos: Luthers Theologie zwischen Mystik und Scholastik* (Tübingen: JCB Mohr, 1972), *passim*.

22. See Gilson, *History of Christian Philosophy*, p. 165.

23. Bernard, *Sermons* XXIV.1.

24. Oberman points out that mysticism was a natural complement to the theological poverty of nominalism: "The usual assumption that nominalism and mysticism are mutually exclusive would therefore no longer seem tenable" (*Harvest of Medieval Theology*, p. 6). See also Ozment, "Mysticism, Nominalism and Dissent," in *The Pursuit of Holiness in Late Medieval and Renaissance Religion*, ed. C. Trinkhaus and H. A. Oberman, Vol. X of the series *Studies in Medieval and Reformation Thought*, pp. 67ff.

25. *WA* 3, p. 124.

26. *LW* 36, p. 109.

27. Many reprints and translations of Bernard's writings are available, including *The Steps to Humility*, ed. G. B. Burch (Cambridge: Harvard University Press, 1950).

28. *WA* 4, p. 111.

29. *Humilitas sola salvat*; *WA* 4, p. 473.

30. See Oberman, *Harvest of Medieval Theology*, p. 359; see also H. A. Oberman, "Gabriel Biel and Late Medieval Mysticism," *Church History*, 30 (1961), pp. 259-287.

31. In disputes among the scholastic *viae*, Gerson sided with nominalism, for the nominalists at least never suggested that many of the arbitrary and useless questions being disputed (i.e., can the Son produce another Son because he is of the same power as the Father?) were more than abstract speculation which ultimately revealed more about the failure of the human intellect than they contributed to knowledge of God. In his *De mystica theologia Speculativa* (1408), Gerson argues that it is precisely where reason finds its limitations -- the point at which a conformity of intellect is found to be impossible -- that the soul meets the Divine. In his attempt to counter the overall effects of the disputations, Gerson introduced the Franciscan theme of the simple imitation of Christ as the true source of wisdom. *Jesum imitari, imitandus est Jesus factus nobis a Deo sapientia.* See Oberman, *Harvest of Medieval Theology*, pp. 331-360, and Gilson, *History of Christian Philosophy*, pp. 524-534.

32. From the ninth chapter on, Luther used Erasmus' recently published New Testament text which he found to be more reliable. However, his *scholia* remains strongly influenced throughout by Stapulensis.

33. Faber Stapulensis, "Introduction to the Commentary on the Psalms," p. 300, reprinted in *Forerunners of the Reformation: The Shape of Late Medieval*

Thought, ed. Heiko A. Oberman (U.S.A.: Holt, Rinehart and Winston, 1966), pp. 297-301.

34. Stapulensis, "Introduction to the Commentary on the Psalms," reprinted in Oberman, ed., *Forerunners of the Reformation*, p. 298.

35. *Ibid.*
Thomas à Kempis in *The Imitation of Christ* writes, "The whole of Holy Scripture has to be read by the Spirit by which it was written. We had better look to Scripture for what is edifying than for precision of language" (Bk. I, Ch. 5). Many editions are available, including *The Imitation of Christ*, trans. B. I. Knott (London: Collins/Fontana, 1963). For a history of the late medieval letter/spirit debate, see Oberman, "The Literal and Spiritual Sense of Scripture," *Forerunners of the Reformation*, pp. 281-296.

36. The concept of the *sacra ignorantia* is found in most branches of mystical theology. See especially the treatise *Of Learned Ignorance* by Nicholas of Cusa (1401-1464).

37. Faber Stapulensis, "Introduction to the Commentary on Paul," p. 303, reprinted in Oberman, ed., *Forerunners of the Reformation*, pp. 302-303.

38. For an analysis of the imitation of Christ in Stapulensis, see H. Dorries, "Calvin and Lefèvre," *Zeitschrift für Kirchengeschichte*, 44 (1925), pp. 544-581.
In a more recent study, John W. Brush points out that Stapulensis' imitation of Christ is "pursued on very different lines from Erasmus' 'Philosophy of Christ.'" For Stapulensis, "Our imitation of Christ is marked by our humility, our ἀπάθεια, our self-naughting, our suffering, our ascetic severity, our poverty." "Lefèvre d'Étaples: Three Phases of His Life and Work," in *Reformation Studies: Essays in Honor of Roland H. Bainton*, ed. Franklin Littell (Richmond: John Knox Press, 1962), p. 126, see also pp. 117-128.

39. See Erich Vogelsang, "Weltbild und Kreuzestheologie in den Hollenfahrtsstreitigkeiten der Reformationszeit," *Archiv für Reformationsgeschichte*, 37 (1940), pp. 90-132.

40. The *resignatio voluntatis* was a rather common concept within late medieval mysticism. Stapulensis may have borrowed it from Johannes Tauler who wrote, "All true blessedness lies in proper resignation and being without a will," as quoted by von Loewenich in *Luther's Theology of the Cross*, p. 158.

41. For an analysis of the influence of Stapulensis on Luther, see Fritz Hahn, "Faber Stapulensis und Luther," *Zeitschrift für Kirchengeschichte*, 57 (1938), pp. 364ff.

42. *WA* 56, p. 375; see also *LW* 42, p. 44.

43. *LW* 2, p. 321.

44. *WA* 3, p. 431.

45. *LW* 14, p. 31; *WA* 4, p. 111.

46. *WA* 3, p. 458; see also *WA* 4, p. 111.

47. See also *LW* 10, p. 122; *WA* 3, p. 126.

48. *WA* 5, p. 176.

49. *LW* 30, p. 110; *WA* 12, p. 364.

50. *WA* 1, p. 32. It should be noted that when Luther refers to 'flesh' it is not intended in the Platonic sense of 'body' but in the Hebraic sense of 'evil heart.'

51. *Ibid.*, p. 32.

52. *WA* 56, p. 380; see also *WA* 56, p. 423.

53. *Ibid.*

54. *WA* 56, p. 391.

55. *WA* 4, p. 110.

56. *Ibid.*

57. *WA* 3, p. 463; *LW* 10, p. 405.

58. *WA* 4, p. 82; *WA* 55 II, p. 106. See John Dillenberger, *God Hidden and Revealed: The Interpretation of Luther's 'Deus Absconditus' and its Significance for Religious Thought* (Philadelphia: Muhlenberg Press, 1953), *passim.*

59. *LW* 10, p. 250.

60. *LW* 25, p. 233.

61. *WA* 3, p. 127.

62. *LW* 31, p. 52.

63. *WA* 56, p. 423.

64. Luther does not explicitly use the term *theologia crucis* until his Hebrews lectures (1517) and Heidelberg Disputation (1518). However the various components which form its content are already present by 1516.

65. The themes of humility, suffering and the hiddenness of God permeated the Germanic mystical tradition. In his appeal to the *theologia crucis/theologia gloriae* distinction, Luther was simply another of a long line of theologians who drew upon the resources of mystical theology for a critique of scholasticism. Despite the significance Walther von Loewenich has attributed to Luther's use of the term *theologia crucis* in the Heidelberg Disputation, it still remains that von Staupitz had requested that Karlstadt, the senior debator, and Luther avoid the more controversial and debatable points, in that they needed support from the other Augustinians. Luther uses the term without feeling the need to explain its use, presumably because it was already understood by his audience. Furthermore, of Luther's 41 propositions condemned by the Bull, *Exsurge Domine*, none touch the theology of the cross. See John Dillenberger's introduction to Luther's "Theses for the *Heidelberg Disputation*," in *Martin Luther: Selections from His Writings* (New York: Doubleday/Anchor Books, 1961), pp. 500-503; and E. Gordon Rupp, "Luther's Ninety-Five Theses and the Theology of the Cross," in *Luther for an Ecumenical Age: Essays in Commemoration of the 450th Anniversary of the Reformation*, ed. Carl S. Meyer (Saint Louis: Concordia, 1967), pp. 67-81; and Heino O. Kadai, "Luther's Theology of the Cross," in *Accents in Luther's Theology: Essays in Commemoration of the 450th Anniversary of the Reformation*, ed. Heino O. Kadai (Saint Louis: Concordia, 1967), pp. 230-272.

66. *LW* 14, p. 152; see also *WA* 56, p. 376, and *LW* 25, p. 75.

67. *LW* 6, p. 151; *WA* 44, p. 113.

68. *LW* 51, p. 15; *WA* 1, p. 111.

69. *LW* 51, p. 18; *WA* 1, p. 115.

70. "Take it and eat; it will be bitter to your stomach but sweet as honey in your mouth" -- Rev. 10:9 (RSV).
   "For the Lord shall rise up ... that he may do his work, his strange work; and bring to pass his act, his strange act" -- Isaiah 28:21 (RSV).

71. *LW* 51, p. 15; *WA* 1, p. 111.

72. *LW* 51, p. 119; *WA* 32, p. 29; see also *LW* 25, p. 112.

73. I Cor. 15:49 -- *LW* 42, pp. 10-11; *WA* 2, p. 138; see also *LW* 31, p. 153.

74. For an analysis of Luther's understanding of conformity to the suffering Christ, see G. Rost, "Der Gedanke der Gleichförmigkeit mit dem lebenden Christus in der Frömmigkeit des jungen Luthers," *Lutherischer Rundblick*, 11 (1963), *passim*.

75. *WA* 1, p. 112; *LW* 51, p. 22; see also George H. Williams, "German Mysticism in the Polarization of Ethical Behavior in Luther and the Anabaptists," *The Mennonite Quarterly Review*, 48 (1974), pp. 284ff.

76. *LW* 42, p. 50; *WA* 2, p. 106.

77. *LW* 2, p. 134; *WA* 42, p. 356.

78. *WA* 56, p. 376.

79. *WA Tr.* 1, p. 117.

80. *LW* 5, p. 50; *WA* 43, p. 463.

81. *LW* 51, p. 19; *WA* 1, p. 111.

IV. *CONFORMITAS CHRISTI*

A.   Johannes Tauler

- 1 -

In 1513, Faber Stapulensis, the mentor of Luther's Psalms commentaries, edited and published a collection of mystical and visionary writings by representatives of the *devotio moderna*[1] and Germanic mystical traditions entitled *Liber trium vigorum et spiritualium virginum.* Among the writings were those of Johannes Tauler (c. 1300-1361), a disciple of Meister Eckhart (c. 1260-1327), a friend of Jan van Ruysbroeck (1293-1381) and a member of the group of mystics known as the 'Friends of God.'[2]

In 1516 Luther discovered an anonymous treatise which he edited and entitled *Eyn theologia Deutsch* and which, at the instigation of Johannes von Staupitz, was to become his first publication.[3]   In his preface to the enlarged complete edition of 1518, Luther wrote, "For me, next to the Bible and Saint Augustine, there has come to my hand no book out of which I have learned more and will learn what God, Christ, man and all things are."[4]   Luther felt that its 'unadorned and unassuming words' were precisely what was lacking in contemporary theology.   Although the actual author was unknown during Luther's time, he mistakenly attributed the work to Johannes Tauler,[5] no doubt because of its many similarities to Tauler's *Sermons* which Luther had also come to read and annotate (1515-1516).[6]

Conformitas Christi

For Luther, scholastic theology had become the private preserve of an educated elite involved in theoretical speculation. In Tauler's writings, on the other hand, Luther reported finding "a more solid and sincere theology than is found in all the scholastic teachers of all the universities or than can be found in their propositions."[7] These words, written into the *resolutiones* of his *Thesis on Indulgences* (1518), illustrates the close relationship between Luther's growing understanding and acceptance of mystical theology and his growing dissent. In Tauler, especially, Luther was to find the resources to move forward on several major issues which to date had remained unresolved.[8]

- 2 -

Luther's *theologia crucis* was originally derived from the tradition of penitential affective mysticism as practised by von Staupitz and Stapulensis. Luther differed from this tradition in the extent to which he assigned the role of grace in conforming the Christian to the will of God as articulated in his discussion of the *opus suum Dei*. Although distinctive of Luther's approach, this aspect as well was not unique to him.

Luther first read of the alien and proper work of God in Tauler's *Sermons*, as he acknowledges in his marginalia.[9] Although Tauler supplied the terminology, the ability to see both suffering and redemption as aspects of grace was Luther's particular contribution. Because the specific content of the concept was Luther's own, Tauler's influence in this regard must be considered as indirect.[10] What we are dealing with here appears to be a common linguistic storehouse of elemental concepts rather than a clear dependency.

A more direct and significant influence concerns Tauler's understanding of *conformitas Christi*. However, Luther was to modify this as well and make it uniquely his own. It is to an examination of Tauler's *conformitas Christi* and

76

the theological and soteriological framework within which it is found that we now turn.

- 3 -

In his *Sermons* Tauler had written:

> The most sublime, the supreme way of (God's) call consists in following, outwardly and inwardly, the loving example of His beloved Son, actively and passively, with the aid of images or in contemplation apart from all images. And whoever imitates this (example) with pure heart and totally, will attain to the highest and sublimest goal.[11]

The 'highest and sublimest goal' for Tauler, as for most mystics, was to reunite the human and Divine in a higher *unio mystica*. Within this *unio mystica*, both likeness (*gelichheit*) and unlikeness (*ungelichheit*) between the human and Divine are transcended in a higher synthesis.[12]

Tauler's understanding of the *unio mystica* has its roots in the tradition of Platonic ascetical mysticism. This tradition had been decisively influenced by those aristocrats of the spiritual life, Dionysius the Areopagite, or Pseudo-Dionysius, and Meister Eckhart.

The cosmological presupposition of this tradition was that the individual simultaneously lives in a world of multiplicity and flux, which is visible to the senses, and in a world of unity, which is not visible to the senses. The invisible world is only available to the upper part of the soul with which it is in constant, although unconscious, contact. The consequence of this metaphysical dualism is that it is only possible to know God, who is the source of unity, meditatively without interference from the knowing subject. It was believed that a penetration into the being of God, resulting in a fusion of the knower and the known, was experientially possible. The entire purpose of the ascetic methodology was the destruction or loss of the self in the attempt to attain an 'essentialist' union with the Divine. The dissolution of individual form which characterizes the *unio mystica* is best illustrated by Bernard's example of the drop of water lost in the wine or Meister Eckhart's example of the drop of wine lost in the sea.

From Eckhart in particular, Tauler learned that the *unio mystica* takes place in "the inmost part and highest part of the soul."[13] This he referred to as the *gemut* or *apex mentis*.[14] It is here that "God and you will be united and blessed in the soul's little spark" (*Fünklein*).[15] The *unio mystica* was possible because the *imago Dei* was said to reside in embryonic form in 'the soul's little spark.' A part of the self, namely the soul, thus shared a common ground of being with the Divine, commonly referred to as the *Seelengrund*.

Tauler generally accepted the mixed liquids simile and absorption imagery of the Platonic mystical tradition's characterization of the *unio mystica* by which "created nothing submerges in the uncreated nothing."[16] He accepted many of their concepts regarding the make-up of the soul which in turn informed his own understanding of the *Seelengrund* and *Fünklein*. However, Tauler also differed in several significant respects from this tradition, not the least of which concerns his understanding of the *synteresis*.

- 4 -

For Tauler, the *synteresis* does not exist naturally in human nature. The image of God is not present and waiting to be rediscovered. Rather, the *imago Dei* exists only as potential within the *Fünklein*, waiting to be restored to human nature. The *synteresis* needs to "become a pure substance which is 'made over.'"[17] Whereas the Dionysian mystical tradition emphasized the destruction or loss of the self in the ecstasy and bliss of absorption into Divinity, Tauler placed the emphasis on overcoming self-will in order to restore the true self to its prefallen nature. It is by means of the 'active and passive, inward and outward' *imitatio Christi* that self-will is overcome and "the image of God is restored to man."[18]

Although Tauler agreed that Christians must attain 'the highest and sublimest goal' of the *unio mystica*, he rejected any direct union with God independent of Christ. Tauler held that it was 'likeness to' (*similitudo*) the Son which leads to the Father. Conformity to the image of Christ therefore takes on a new spiritual significance, but this *conformitas* remains distinct and penultimate from any ultimate or 'essentialist' *unio mystica*.[19] In Tauler, Luther found a Christological orientation distinct from that advocated by the medieval scholastic traditions. Its unique feature was that, while the understanding of the *unio mystica* remained theocentric, the understanding of *conformitas* was Christocentric -- a *conformitas Christi* rather than a *conformitas Dei*.

The function of the 'active and passive, inward and outward' imitation of Christ was part of the 'human preparatory activity.' By means of the voluntarily imitative efforts of the Christian carried out 'in pure heart and totally,' the Christian attains a degree of *similitudo*. The Christian is made 'conformable' to Christ. But this is only half of the equation. As mentioned previously, the *synteresis* needs to be 'made over.' The image of God needs to be restored to human nature. The essential and comprehensive nature of the required transformation is not attainable solely on the basis of human effort and preparation. The more significant aspect of Tauler's *conformitas Christi* was its dimension of spiritual significance -- his so-called Christ-mysticism.

According to Tauler, for the *imago Dei* to be restored to the *synteresis*, the birth of Christ in the soul is required. While the imitation of Christ helps to create the precondition of *similitudo* necessary for conformity to occur, it is ultimately the living Christ who takes form in the Christian, conforming the Christian to himself. The imitation of Christ is the necessary preparation for the reception of the *gestalt Christi*. Christ takes form in the soul, replacing the self's orientation with that of Christ. While for scholasticism, the *synteresis* represented an indestructible orientation toward God and the good, for Tauler it was a unique receptacle for the Divine in the depths of the soul. Christians must be passive and resign themselves to the conforming activity of Christ. A degree of selflessness and resignation or *Gelassenheit* is required in order that Christ can become the new transformational centre of the self. The traditional mystical understanding of a graded ascent, therefore, plays only a minor or restricted preparatory role. *Conformitas Christi* entailed not only the ascent of the soul, but more significantly, the descent of God in Christ. Humanity's preparatory ascent meets God's gracious descent.

B. Luther and Tauler

- 1 -

In Tauler, Luther recognized a kindred spirit also stressing the demand for the entire self to conform to the will of God as revealed in 'the loving example of His beloved Son.' In Tauler, Luther saw displayed 'a concern for the spirit,' a concern for the inner life, a concern for the *imitatio mentis*, rather than the moralistic tasks of the *imitatio operis* alone. What was distinctive about Tauler's understanding of *conformitas Christi*, and that aspect of his thought which was to be of greatest importance to Luther's own development, was Tauler's Christ-mysticism.

While Luther was significantly influenced by Tauler's Christ-mysticism and adapted it as the basis of his own understanding of *conformitas Christi*, this is not to suggest his outright acceptance of Tauler's mystical theology. There was, of course, a *sic et non* dimension to Luther's relationship with Tauler.[20]

In general, Luther rejected the Platonic ontological and cosmological elements of Tauler's thought which had been decidedly influenced by Meister Eckhart and the tradition of Areopagitical mysticism. However, even those aspects of Tauler's thought specifically adopted by Luther were adapted to suit the purposes of his own developing theology.

For example, with Tauler, Luther believed that "Christ is the ladder by which we come to the Father (Genesis 28:12)."[21] However, to an even greater extent than Tauler, Luther believed that the ladder to heaven is not one we are capable of climbing but one Christ descended in order to reach out to a sinful humanity. Christ is the *Christus donum*, given to us as a gift in order to help us. In his commentary on Galatians 4:19 Luther relies on Paul to support his stance.

> 'Until Christ be formed in you!' Note Paul's careful choice of words ... as he ascribes more to the grace of God than to his own works .... Neither did he say, 'until you are formed in Christ.' No, his words are 'until Christ be formed in you,' because the Christian's life is not his own; it is Christ's, who lives in him ....[22]

For Luther, the desire to be as God (*homo deificatus*) is the root of all sin.[23] However, Luther also held that our transformation into Christ's likeness is nevertheless the goal of all God's gracious activity toward us. *Conformitas Christi* represents to Luther the process of becoming like Christ or of 'putting on the image of Christ,' not by striving to be Christ-like, but solely by means of the activity of Christ and the Holy Spirit.[24] This position, Luther believed, was also more in line with the original Pauline conception of *conformitas*.

It is not our works but the work of God which makes us conformable to Christ. It is not our righteousness but the righteousness of Christ which makes us acceptable to God. *Conformitas Christi* is not the result of human preparatory activity but is granted to us *sola gratia*.

Luther's acceptance and adaptation of Tauler's Christ-mysticism shifted his understanding of *conformitas* from that of a self-initiated conformity of the will to a theocentric reality (*conformitas voluntatis Dei*) to that of a God-initiated conformity to a Christocentric reality (*conformitas Christi*). However, Luther's rejection of any attempt to initiate righteousness on the basis of an innate goodness claimed by either the agent or on behalf of works, in favour of *sola gratia*, provided the point of his divergence with Tauler's understanding of *conformitas Christi*.

In the penitential mystical tradition, conformity to the image of Christ was attained by stoically resigning oneself to mortification. It was the inherent righteousness of the self (*synteresis*) which provided the resources required to endure purgation, whether the suffering was self-imposed or not. If one persevered in the righteousness provided by the *synteresis* in co-operation with God's grace, salvation would ultimately be granted. The *resignatio voluntatis* and *synteresis* were interrelated and necessary aspects of the process of salvation.

In Tauler, as well, the *synteresis* and *Gelassenheit* were essentially interrelated. But, as pointed out, the self does not possess righteousness as an inherent natural attribute. For Tauler, it is by means of our preparatory activity together with God's gracious descent in Christ that righteousness is restored as an attribute of human nature. It is God in Christ who has taken the initiative. For all intents and purposes then, it is not we who conform ourselves to Christ; rather it is Christ who conforms us to himself.

Nevertheless, it still remains that Christians have the option of co-operating with grace in allowing (*Gelassenheit*) Christ to conform us to himself. Thus while Tauler advocated an essentially different conception of the *ordo salutis*, which denied natural righteousness and allowed a greater role for grace and the work of Christ, he still retained essentially the same understanding of the self's ability to cooperate with grace as had the other medieval traditions. Ultimately, the understanding of the restored or acquired righteousness of the born-again *synteresis* and its corollary, *Gelassenheit*, as advocated by Tauler, is no different from the understanding of the natural righteousness of the *synteresis* and its corollary, the *resignatio voluntatis*, as advocated by Stapulensis.

These similarities are not surprising given the fact that Stapulensis stands in the tradition of Tauler. What this means, however, is that many of Luther's previously outlined criticisms of Stapulensis are also applicable to Tauler.

In both cases, whether the *synteresis* is natural or acquired, the *resignatio* or *Gelassenheit* provide the self with the ability to retain control over the flow of grace and, by implication, the process of salvation. The speculative postulating of the *synteresis* must therefore be seen to pervert a proper understanding of *Gelassenheit*, just as the concept of the *resignatio voluntatis* had led to a perverse understanding of the spiritual value of self-initiated suffering and ascetic practices. The *synteresis*, together with its corollary concepts of *Gelassenheit* and the *resignatio voluntatis*, are ultimately incompatible with a theology of grace.

Furthermore, given that the *synteresis* is the speculative attempt to attribute to the self the power and ability to control and determine the operation of grace and the process of salvation, it follows that neither the *resignatio voluntatis* nor *Gelassenheit* can be said to fulfill the requirements of the *via contrarii* which Luther advocated. God remains ever hidden under the form of contrary appearance as revealed by the cross of Christ. Christ teaches us by his example that death and sin are not overcome by the power and strength of the will which allow us to withstand suffering, as stressed especially by the *resignatio voluntatis*, but by a simple trust in God's grace in the midst of our own sense of weakness, powerlessness and infirmity. Only a proper understanding of faith allows us to accept humbly the route of suffering God has shown us in Christ's death on the cross and to see in it the grace of God. "Faith is the conviction of things not seen."[25]

Conformitas Christi

Suffering must not be seen as the meritorious precondition for *conformitas Christi* but rather as the context in which a life of faith is lived. The stoic endurance of restricted, transient, self-imposed, self-chosen, self-initiated or allegorical suffering on the basis of the righteousness of the *synteresis*, whether natural or acquired, does not represent true faith. Just as the *resignatio voluntatis* and *Gelassenheit* are incompatible with a theology of grace, the *synteresis* is incompatible with a theology of faith. Into his marginal notes to Tauler's *Sermons*[26] Luther wrote that the definitive mark of *homo spiritualis* is not the "affective *synteresis*," but *fides*.[27] After this notation, the *synteresis*, the *resignatio voluntatis* and *Gelassenheit* and the *opus alienum et proprium Dei* were to pass out of Luther's theological vocabulary, replaced entirely by *sola fide, sola gratia* as the basis for *conformitas Christi*.[28]

For Luther, *sola fide* had replaced suffering as the basis of the personal and mystical relationship between Christ and the Christian although suffering remains as the context within which Christ meets us. Humility and suffering are related to *conformitas Christi* as John the Baptist is related to Christ, not as the precondition or cause of Christ's coming but as expectation and fulfillment. When our righteousness is revealed as unrighteousness, all that is left is to turn to faith in Christ and trust in God's loving, gracious activity.

C. *Sola Fide*

- 1 -

For Tauler, *conformitas Christi* was anticipated and in part instigated by the 'human preparatory activity' of the 'inward and outward, active and passive' *imitatio Christi*. We initiate a condition of *similitudo* such that Christ can take form in us, conforming us to himself.

Luther agreed with Tauler that righteousness is not possessed *naturaliter*, but must be attained, or more accurately, granted by God. Luther also agreed with Tauler that it is Christ who conforms us to himself. However, unlike Tauler, for Luther *conformitas Christi* represented the rejection of any and all anthropological or volitional unitive principles. On this basis, he was to reject the prescriptive aspect of Tauler's imitation of Christ, at least to the degree that it still represented a *theologia gloriae* in its assertion that the self-initiated attainment of *similitudo* is the precondition for *conformitas Christi*.[29]

Humanity and God are related as darkness is to light and not as light is to light. The believer's relationship to Christ is 'a coincidence of opposites' such that it is only possible to say "'I am Christ' because Christ has first said to me 'I am that sinner.'"[30] We do not ascend; rather it is through Christ's descent that it is possible to be conformed to Christ. We are conformed to Christ not as a consequence of our preparatory attempts to become 'like' Christ, but solely by means of Christ's gracious activity. Luther writes, "The whole procedure of justification is passive."[31]

In the place of the imitation of Christ, Luther placed the pre-eminence of faith. *Conformitas Christi* is a communion of faith in which the Divine / human encounter is bridged by the activity of the Holy Spirit such that one can say with Paul, "It is no longer I who lives but Christ who lives in me."[32] Faith in Christ means "putting on Christ and having all things in common with Him."[33] It is faith which carries us "into those things which can be neither inwardly nor outwardly experienced."[34] It is faith which "conjoins the soul with Christ like a bride with her bridegroom."[35] It is faith alone which makes of the believer and Christ "as one person."[36] For Luther, faith in Christ and *conformitas Christi* had become interchangeable terms.[37]

As *conformitas Christi* has its source outside of us, faith must also be seen as a gift of grace rather than as engendered from within. True faith does not permit us to claim any righteousness for ourselves. Otherwise the temptation may be to see faith itself as a good and meritorious work and a basis for receiving righteousness. True faith is not granted to us on the basis of our aptitudes or attributes but on the basis of Christ's sacrificial death. Faith in Christ, properly understood as itself the gift of the Holy Spirit, is the only form of relationship with Christ not infected by self-righteous claims.

- 2 -

While Luther declared that his theology was a product of the "wisdom of experience,"[38] he often speaks of a realm beyond experience. Luther's Christ-mysticism stressed the pneumatic presence of the crucified and risen Christ in the Christian -- "the spiritual birth of the incarnate Word"[39] -- rather than merely a psychological presence or the speculative presence of the *synteresis* as conceived by various medieval schools. To Luther, *conformitas Christi* signifies a contemporaneousness in life and destiny rather than merely in knowing, willing or feeling. *Conformitas Christi* occurs beyond reason, perception or conscious awareness. It is a hidden life so deep and profound that it remains hidden even from oneself. *Conformitas Christi* occurs in the depths of the self, accomplished *in mysterium*, as a gift of the Holy Spirit.[40]

With Tauler, Luther emphasized that *conformitas Christi* is the result of the indwelling of Christ within the believer -- a *mystica incarnatio*.[41] Christ takes form in the Christian conforming the Christian to himself. Christ becomes our new centre by which we are made aware of the pervasive effect of sin upon and in our nature. Christ is the *Christus donum*, given to us to help us in our struggle against 'the old Adam,' forcing the 'outer man' to "obey and conform to the inner man."[42]

Furthermore, Luther held that *conformitas Christi* is the locus of the 'wonderful' or 'happy exchange' of *iustitia* and *peccata* between Christ and the Christian, by which Christ takes upon himself the sins of the believer and the believer receives the righteousness of Christ.[43] Luther writes, "Our sins are now not ours but Christ's, and Christ's righteousness is not Christ's but ours."[44]

Unlike Tauler, Luther did not believe that Christ is present in the *synteresis*. The *imago Dei* is not restored to human nature. Righteousness is not an attribute we can claim as our own. Our righteousness is solely the righteousness of Christ and therefore cannot be said to exist *in re*.[45] The righteousness by which we are reckoned as righteous before God is not an infused righteousness but an 'alien righteousness' which is shared and held only in faith.[46] To claim any righteousness for ourselves, whether natural or acquired, is to surrender one's faith and with it the true righteousness provided by Christ's sacrificial death.

Although we are 'made over' in our struggle against the sinner, although "we have 'put on Christ' as the role of righteousness and our salvation,"[47] we are and continue to be "partly sinners and partly righteous."[48] The Christian remains *incurvatus in se* but in faith is also *ingressus in Christus*. Both realities coexist, with the one realm providing the boundary and limitation of the other.[49] The faithful are righteous in that they are accepted as righteous before God for the sake of Christ's sacrificial death, but the faithful can see themselves only as sinners.[50] Everything positive in the Christian life remains hidden under negation. Only in faith is one grasped by the alien righteousness of Christ. Only when grasped by the alien righteousness of Christ is it possible to recognize oneself as a sinner and confess that 'I do evil'; and only when grasped by the alien righteousness of Christ is it possible to "hate the evil that I do."[51] By faith alone is it possible to be *simul iustus et peccator*. By faith alone is it possible to acknowledge that "A Christian is at the same time righteous and sinner, saint and profane, enemy and Son of God."[52]

NOTES

1. The *devotio moderna* was a spiritual movement originating in the Low Countries toward the end of the 14th century. Central to the movement was a burgeoning lay group known as the 'Brethren of the Common Life.' The group was originally founded by Gerhard Groote (1340-1384) and organized by his friend and successor, Florens Radewijns (1350-1400) into religious communities modelled on those of the primitive Church. The movement was carried by a fervour of idealism which required Papal warnings as it spread throughout Germany and central Europe during the 15th century. The Brethren originally desired to be recognized as a new order but could not be accredited as the Lateran Council (1215) had forbidden the recognition of new orders.

See R. R. Post, *The Modern Devotion: Confrontation with Reformation and Humanism*, Vol. III of the series *Studies in Medieval and Reformation Thought*, ed. H. A. Oberman (Leiden: E. J. Brill, 1968), *passim*; and E. Iserloh, "The *Devotio Moderna*," in *Handbook of Church History*, IV, pp. 426-443; and A. Hyma, *The Christian Renaissance: A History of the "Devotio Moderna"* (Hamden, Connecticut: Archon Books, 1965). See also T. P. van Zyl, *Gerhard Groote: Ascetic and Reformer* (Washington: Catholic University of America Press, 1963); and A. D. Bos, "Gerhard Groote (1340-1384) and the Brothers of the Common Life: An Experiment for Today?," *Cithara*, 15 (1976).

The movement was well known to Luther from the time when, as a youngster, he had 'attended school with the Brethren in Magdeburg.' Other members or Brethren-trained people who were to have an influence upon Luther included Gabriel Biel, Peter d'Ailly, Johannes Popper von Goch and Wesel Gansfort.

For an analysis of the function of the imitation of Christ in the *devotio moderna*, see E. Iserloh, "Die Kirchenfrömmigkeit in der *Imitatio Christi*," in *Sentire Ecclesiam*, ed. J. Daniélou and A. Vorgrémler (Freiburg: Herder, 1961), pp. 251-267.

2. In 1329 Pope John XXII condemned 28 of Eckhart's propositions (17 as heretical and 11 as rash and suspect). Eckhart's popularily proved stronger than the interdicts of the Church and a line of confrontation was drawn between Eckhart's followers and the Church. Those who chose to follow Eckhart's teaching founded a loose association of like-minded individuals who came to be known as the Friends of God. The condemnation of the Church indirectly helped to shape their theology. Deprived of the sacraments they came to believe that they were not thereby excluded from the presence of God; rather they saw themselves as the true Church within a corrupt Christendom. Other members of the Friends included Heinrich Suso (c. 1300-1366) and Rulman Merswin (1307-1382). See E. Iserloh, "The German Mystics," in *Handbook of Church History*, IV, pp. 375-390.

3. Luther's first edition of 1516, containing Chapters VI-XXVI of the original, was actually entitled *A Spiritually Noble Little Book*. It did not receive its more recognizable title until the complete edition of 1518. Several versions are available in English translation. The one based on the manuscript of 1497 which Luther used is available as *Theologia Germanica: The Way of a Sinless Life*, ed. T. S. Kepler (New York: The World Publishing Co., 1952). For an analysis of the history and influence of *Eyn Theologia Deutsch*, see Steven E. Ozment, *Mysticism and Dissent: Religious Ideology and Social Protest in the Sixteenth Century* (New Haven: Yale University Press, 1973), *passim*.

4. *WA* 1, p. 378.

5. *WA* 7, pp. 152-153. Based upon a reference in the edition of 1497, the work is now known to be the product of a member of the Teutonic Knights of Sachsenhausen near Frankfurt in the latter half of the 14th century, who had himself been strongly influenced by Johannes Tauler.

6. Luther used the 1508 Augsburg edition of Tauler's *Sermons* which contained 84 sermons. The principle collection of Tauler's *Sermons* available in English translation is that of S. Dinkworth, *The History and Life of the Reverend Doctor John Tauler with Twenty-Five of His Sermons* (London: n.d.). Another Deutero-Taulerian work, also mistakenly attributed to Tauler, with which Luther was familiar, was the *Nachfolgung des armen Lebens Jesu Christi*. This work is available in English translation as *The Book of the Poor in Spirit by a Friend of God (Fourteenth Century): A Guide to Rhineland Mysticism*, ed. C. F. Kelly (New York: 1954).

7. *LW* 31, p. 129; *WA* 1, p. 557.

8. Some theologians have cast Luther's relationship with mystical theology in contrasting and antithetical terms although due to recent scholarship this has been changing. Walther von Loewenich, for example, in his first edition of *Luther's Theologia Crucis* (München: Chr. Kaiser Verlag, 1929) assumed an absolute opposition between Luther and Tauler. By the fourth edition of 1954, this position was significantly reevaluated and entire sections on Luther's relationship to Tauler added. However von Loewenich and others continued to argue that although mysticism may have had an influence upon Luther's early career, this influence was to cease after 1520. Gerhard Ebeling, for one, claims that Luther "withdrew from his admiration of the German theologian (*Theologia Germanica*) and Tauler already in 1520" (*Luther: An Introduction to His Thought* (Great Britain: Collins, 1970)). Heiko Oberman, on the other hand, argues that there are many references of a positive nature of Johannes Tauler and Bernard of Clairvaux long after 1520. See Heiko A. Oberman, "*Simul Gemitus et Raptus*: Luther und die Mystik," in *The Church, Mysticism, Sanctification and the Natural in Luther's Thought: Lectures Presented to the Third International Congress on*

Luther Research, Järvendää, Finland August 11-16, 1966, ed. Ivar Asheim (Philadelphia: Fortress Press, 1967), pp. 37ff. See also Bengt R. Hoffman, *Luther and the Mystics* (Minneapolis: Augsburg Pub., 1976), *passim*.

9. *WA* 9, pp. 95ff.

10. See Paul Althaus, *The Theology of Martin Luther* (Philadelphia: Fortress Press, 1966), pp. 21ff.

11. Johannes Tauler, *Predigten* 53, as quoted by Iserloh, *Handbook of Church History*, IV, p. 382.

12. See Ozment, *Homo Spirituulis*, pp. 8-9, 45 56 for an analysis of Tauler's understanding of the *unio mystica* and its anthropological foundation.

13. Tauler, *Predigten*, as quoted by Iserloh, *Handbook of Church History*, IV, p. 379.

14. See Williams, "German Mysticism and the Polarization of Ethical Behaviour," p. 279; and Ozment, *Homo Spiritualis*, pp. 99-101.

15. Tauler, *Predigten*, as quoted by Iserloh, *Handbook of Church History*, IV, p. 383.

16. Tauler, *Predigten*, as quoted by von Loewenich, *Luther's Theology of the Cross*, p. 154.

17. Tauler, *Predigten*, as quoted by Hägglund, *The Background of Luther's Doctrine of Justification in Late Medieval Theology* in *Facet Books Historical Series*, 18, ed. G. S. Anderson (Philadelphia: Fortress Press, 1961), p. 12.

18. Tauler, *Predigten*, as quoted by Hägglund, *The Background of Luther's Doctrine of Justification in Late Medieval Theology* in G. S. Anderson, ed., *Facet Books Historical Series*, 18, p. 12.

19. See Ozment, *Homo Spiritualis*, pp. 36-44.

20. See Oberman, *"Simul Gemitus et Raptus*: Luther und die Mystik," pp. 24-28. Cf. also Iserloh, "Luther und die Mystik," pp. 60-83; and Bengt Hägglund, "Luther und die Mystik," in *Church, Mysticism, Sanctification and the Natural in Luther's Thought*, pp. 84-94.

21. *LW* 36, p. 109.

22. *LW* 27, pp. 308-309; *WA* 2, p. 548. "My little children, with whom I am again in travail until Christ be formed in you" -- Galatians 4:19 (RSV).

23. *WA* 3, p. 498.

24. For an analysis of the role played by the Holy Spirit in the process of *conformitas Christi*, see Prenter, *Spiritus Creator*, pp. 9-11 and 27.

25. *LW* 17, p. 13; *WA* 22 II, p. 364.

26. Marginal notes to Sermon 52, *WA* 9, pp. 103ff.

27. For an explanation of the significance of this notation, see Erwin Iserloh, "Luther's Christ-Mysticism," in *Catholic Scholars Dialogue with Luther*, ed. Jared Wicks (Chicago: Loyola University Press, 1970), pp. 43ff.; see also Ozment, "Luther and the Late Middle Ages: Formation of Reformation Thought," pp. 128ff.

28. See Williams, "German Mysticism and the Polarization of Ethical Behaviour," p. 283.

29. See von Loewenich, *Luther's Theology of the Cross*, pp. 152-159.

30. *WA* 40 I, p. 285.

31. *WA* 40 II, p. 410.

32. Galatians 2:20.

33. *WA* 2, p. 504.

34. *WA* 57 III, p. 149.

35. *WA* 7, p. 25. Although Luther rejected the nuptial imagery used by the Dionysian/Eckhardian tradition to describe the relationship between God and the soul (cf. *WA* 39 I, p. 389), he uses the same language to describe the relationship between Christ and the faithful. An important difference is that Luther's stress was never on the *unio mystica*. It was not the ecstacy of divine union that mattered to Luther but the blessedness accessible to all the faithful.

36. *Quasi unam personam*. *WA* 40 I, p. 285; *LW* 26, p. 168.

37. This point is well documented by Regin Prenter. According to Prenter, "the idea of conformity is insolubly united with (Luther's) concept of faith. *Conformitas Christi* and *fides Christi* are identical. It was only late Lutheranism

that began to speak about a faith that was separated from the real conformity with Christ in his death and resurrection." *Spiritus Creator*, p. 167; see also p. 50.

38. *Sapientia experimentalis (non doctrinalis)*; WA 11, p. 98.

39. *WA* 9, p. 98.

40. It is this retention of a realm of *mysterium* which ultimately makes it difficult to find precedents to Luther in the other medieval 'isms' which sought to illuminate that which is hidden from us rather than having the faith to accept that which is hidden.

41. Prenter, *Spiritus Creator*, p. 11.

42. *LW* 31, p. 358.

43. *Fröhlicher wechsel* -- see *WA* 1, p. 593, *LW* 31, pp. 189ff.; *WA* 7, p. 25; *WA* 7, p. 54, *LW* 31, p. 351; *WA* 31 II, p. 435.

44. *WA* 5, p. 608.

45. *In spe non in re* -- *WA* 3, p. 363; see also Joseph Lortz, "The Basic Elements of Luther's Intellectual Style," in *Catholic Scholars Dialogue with Luther*, p. 15.

46. *Aliena iustitia* -- see *WA* 27, p. 146, *WA* 2, pp. 145ff., *LW* 31, pp. 297ff.; *WA* 2, p. 491, *LW* 27, p. 222; *WA* 39 I, p. 83, *LW* 34, p. 153; *WA* 39 I, p. 109, *LW* 34, p. 178; *WA* 46, p. 44, *LW* 24, p. 347.

47. *LW* 27, p. 128.

48. *WA* 40 II, p. 86; *LW* 27, p. 68; see also *WA* 56, p. 70.

49. Luther sometimes uses *partim* terminology when speaking of the relationship between sinner and righteous (*WA* 40 II, p. 86; *LW* 27, p. 68) while at other times he speaks in terms of two totalities -- *totus iustus, totus peccator* (*WA* 39 I, pp. 563-664). Both forms of terminology attempt to emphasize a mutual qualification. See also *WA* 56, p. 70; *WA* 57, p. 165; *WA* 2, pp. 496ff., *LW* 27, pp. 230ff.; *WA* 38, p. 205; *WA* 40 II, p. 352, *LW* 12, p. 328; *WA* 8, p. 67, *LW* 32, p. 173.

50. *LW* 27, p. 21; *WA* 40 II, p. 1; see also *WA* 56, p. 423.

51. *WA* 56, p. 70.

52. *WA* 40 I, p. 368.

V. SACRAMENTUM ET EXEMPLUM

A. Luther and Augustine

- 1 -

Luther originally accepted Biel's formulation of the *conformitas voluntatis et rationis Dei*. The influence of Paul, Augustine and Stapulensis made a greater Christological orientation available to Luther, leading him further from an understanding of *conformitas Dei* toward an understanding which had as its objective conformity with the image of the Son of God. Eventually, with the influence of Tauler's Christ-mysticism, Luther came to the development of his own unique understanding of *conformitas Christi*. However, at the centre of Luther's growing Christological orientation was a significantly reformulated Christology.

Ever since Bernard of Clairvaux boldly proclaimed, "I do not see Christ as accessible only to my prayers, but I dare even to imitate Him,"[1] the humanity of Jesus had grown in Christological importance. Both scholasticism and nominalism (as represented by Biel), and Germanic mystical theology (as represented by Tauler), maintained an *imitatio Christi* methodology. Whether the particular form was that of an *imitatio operis* (*obedientia activa*) or an *imitatio mentis* (*obedientia passiva*) or some combination thereof, the Christological emphasis was placed upon the *Christus exemplum* -- Christ as the archetypal and paradigmatic example for Christians to imitate.

Sacramentum et Exemplum

Augustine, the *Doctor gratiae*, provided Luther with more than his anti-Pelagian thesis. He also provided him with a new Christological formulation which made it possible for Luther to come to terms with the emphasis upon the *Christus exemplum* which dominated the construction of late medieval Christologies. Augustine's Christology included not only the *Christus exemplum*, but also the *Christus sacramentum* -- Christ as the sign that God had acted for our salvation through the sacrifice and death of Christ for the sins of humanity.[2]

Luther makes note of the *sacramentum et exemplum* Christology for the first time in his marginalia to Augustine's *De Trinitate* (Book IV, Ch. III) upon which he lectured in 1509 and from which the concept was originally borrowed.[3] The *sacramentum et exemplum* appears throughout his Psalms lectures although always in reference to Augustine.[4] It is in his lectures on Romans and Hebrews that the *sacramentum et exemplum* is finally appropriated by Luther for his own purposes and becomes firmly entrenched in his thought.[5]

- 2 -

The traditional medieval interpretation of Romans and Hebrews, using the tools of literal and tropological or moral exegesis, was that the death and resurrection of Christ are examples of what Christians must undergo as well. Luther's original conception of conformity to the image of Christ also placed great emphasis upon the *Christus exemplum*. However by the time of his *Lectures on Romans*, Luther uses the *sacramentum et exemplum* Christology specifically in order to exclude a superficially moralistic understanding of the death and resurrection of Christ. Referring specifically to Romans 6:4,[6] Luther writes, "the apostle speaks here of the death and resurrection of Christ inasmuch as they are *sacramentum* and not inasmuch as they are *exemplum*."[7] From this time onward these were understood by Luther, not so much as an example of a truly Christian life, as they are a sign that in Christ God had already acted for us.

If the *Christus exemplum* is stressed to the virtual exclusion of the *Christus sacramentum*, the danger is of reducing Christ to a prophet and the Gospel into law. Luther writes: "You must not make a Moses out of Christ as if He did no more than teach and give an example as the other saints do, as if the Gospel were a book of instruction and laws."[8] From the perspective of Augustine's *sacramentum et exemplum* Christological formulation, Luther could question the apparent reduction of Christology to the example of Christ, which together with the *synteresis* placed the initiative for salvation in human hands and the means of salvation in human works.

In the Hebrews commentary as well, while Luther continues to emphasize the *Christus exemplum*, our attention is often drawn to the *Christus sacramentum*. Referring to Hebrews 10:19-22, Luther writes:

> Not only does Christ show us the way, He also holds out His hand
> for those who are following .... Christ alone is not only our
> companion on the way, but also our leader, and not only our leader
> but also our helper, in fact He carries us over.[9]

This is a significant departure from the medieval exegesis of Hebrews 10:19-22 which stressed primarily the exemplary nature of Christ's death and Christ's preventient function as 'leader' rather than Christ's providential function as 'helper' and significance as *sacramentum*.[10]

In his commentary on Hebrews, Luther points out what he believes to be the error of medieval Christology and establishes the basis for his own Christology. Luther acknowledges that while the life, works and death of Christ serve an important exemplary function, the need for, and significance of, the *Christus sacramentum* is paramount and should never be minimized. Both the *sacramentum et exemplum* are essential for a truly Christian life. Luther writes:

> (T)hose people make a huge mistake who first try to block out
> their sins by good works and penitential practices, for they try to
> begin with Christ as *exemplum* when they ought to begin with Him
> as *sacramentum*.[11]

Sacramentum et Exemplum

Luther's criticism of the works-righteousness, meritoriousness and soteriological significance attributed to the imitation of Christ, together with the development of his *sola fide, sola gratia* soteriological stance, led him to his new and unique understanding of the function of the *sacramentum et exemplum*. More than simply stressing both aspects of the one reality of Christ, Luther takes it one step further -- he maintains that Christ's sacramental significance has priority over his exemplary significance. The example of Christ is a derivative function, dependent and based upon the primacy of the *Christus sacramentum*. In fact, the example of Christ is significant only as a consequence of Christ's sacramental function. What Christ has done before us as *exemplum* has meaning and validity only because of what Christ has done for us as *sacramentum*.

- 3 -

It was never the case, of course, that medieval theology stressed the *Christus exemplum* to the exclusion of the *Christus sacramentum*, just as it was never the case that 'good works' performed in imitation of Christ without an accompanying *infusio gratia* would lead to righteousness. In Luther's judgment, however, the cultivation of 'good works' and the *Christus exemplum* had curtailed an acknowledgement of the efficaciousness of the *sacramentum*, or had reduced its significance to a 'minute motion,' as in Gabriel Biel.

For Biel, Christ's death on the cross was expiatory only in regard to a relatively narrow conception of *peccatum originale.*[12] It was primarily the culmination of a life dedicated to obedience to God's will and the active fulfillment of righteousness. The death itself seems almost incidental.[13]

For Luther, on the other hand, sin was all pervasive, applying not only to works but to all of human nature. Luther charged that Biel's doctrine of justification, with its exaggerated dependence on an *actum meritorium* to make us acceptable to God, fails to recognize the deeper dimensions of sin and excludes Christ himself as our righteousness and faith in him as the condition of our justification.[14] It is by his blood that Christ has effected a reconciliation between God and humanity.[15] The cross of Christ is not the inevitable end but the beginning of a truly Christian life.

As Anselm (1033-1109) before him, Luther viewed Christ's death as satisfaction for the sins of humanity. Christ took the sins of humanity upon himself and in this sense stood before God as a substitutionary sinner satisfying God's wrath for our sins.[16] However, unlike Anselm's doctrine of the Atonement, Luther held that the term 'satisfaction' is "too weak to fully express the grace of Christ and does not adequately honour his suffering."[17] For Luther, Christ has not only taken our sins upon his shoulders but continues to do so. Christ is the "eternal satisfaction for our sin."[18]

Luther's use of the term *Christus sacramentum* includes not only the element of eternal satisfaction but is also meant to express the personal appropriation of Christ's vicarious satisfaction by the faithful. It is by means of the mediational activity of the Holy Spirit that Jesus Christ is taken out of the remoteness of history and heavenly exaltation and placed, by means of the sacraments, into the midst of the Christian life as a living reality conforming us to himself.[19] However, in order to undertand Luther in this regard, it is important not to cast the *sacramentum* in narrow dogmatic conceptualizations as the Eucharistic debates of the late medieval and reformation periods were prone to do.

The significant feature of Luther's notion of *sacramentum* is that Christ is truly present in the seemingly insignificant and lowly things of this world. The sacraments in and of themselves mean little to Luther, for that which they signify (i.e., the assurance of grace as promised in the Gospels) is granted always to those who have faith.[20] The sign points beyond itself to the promise of the forgiveness of sins and God's unconditional love for humanity. In this sense, Christ himself is also a sacrament if understood properly as the incarnation of God who has affected our salvation through his redemptive passion.[21]

Sacramentum et Exemplum

In both cases, whether the *Christus sacramentum* is understood as Christ's sacrifice or as the Holy Spirit-mediated presence of Christ in the sacraments, both are a God-given sign that God is present and active in the midst of life. In both cases, in relying wholly and solely on the faith that Christ has already won the victory on our behalf, the Holy Spirit grants us the joyful confidence and assurance of salvation. The discussion of isolated Christological and liturgical formulas and rites can obscure this profound and dynamic dimension of Luther's understanding of the nature of the *Christus sacramentum*.

B. *Fides Christus Sacramentum, Imitatio Christus Exemplum*

- 1 -

Awareness of Luther's development of *sola fide, sola gratia*, the *Christus sacramentum* and *conformitas Christi*, together with his rejection of the *synteresis* and the meritorious and soteriological significance of good works, has led some historians and interpreters of Luther to conclude that Luther's critique of the imitation of Christ and the example of Christ constitutes a wholesale rejection of them in his thought. Consequently, they argue, as does the Finnish scholar Lennart Pinomaa, for the antithetical relationship between the *sacramentum et exemplum* and *conformitas Christi* and *imitatio Christi*. Pinomaa writes:

> Already in his early evangelical theology, where those thoughts are found, Luther rejects the idea that Christ is primarily our example. Gradually the alternatives become clear to him: either *Christus exemplum* (Christ the example) or *Christus sacramentum* (Christ as the sacrifice for us). With Christ as our example, we end up in despair, as God's gift to us he is our life and salvation. Luther indeed speaks of Christ as our example, but not one we have to imitate; for it is God Himself who conforms us to Christ's likeness.[22]

98

Against the great emphasis placed upon human abilities, albeit in cooperation with the grace of God, it was only natural that Luther would stress faith and Christ's atoning sacrifice in his criticism of the works-righteousness and soteriological significance associated with the practice of the imitation of Christ as advocated by many of his predecessors and contemporaries. Within this context, faith in Christ's sacrifice indeed stands in sharp contrast to the imitation of Christ. However, although Luther stressed faith in Christ's salvific death on the cross as the soteriologically significant Christological event, his intention was never to exclude the imitation of the example of Christ, as Pinomaa and others maintain.[23]

In his 1519 commentary on Galatians 2:20, for example, Luther explains Paul's phrase "with Christ I have been crucified," in reference to Augustine and the *sacramentum et exemplum* Christology.

> Saint Augustine teaches that the suffering Christ is both a *sacramentum* and an *exemplum*, -- a *sacramentum* because it signifies the death of sin in us and grants it to those who believe, an *exemplum* because it also behooves us to imitate Him in bodily suffering and dying.[24]

In his explanation of Paul's phrase "putting on Christ" (Gal. 3:27), Luther explains that it is not only Christ's suffering that is to be imitated but his virtues and works as well. Luther writes:

> Putting on Christ is understood in two ways: according to the Law and according to the Gospel. According to the Law (Rom. 13:14), 'Put on the Lord Jesus Christ'; that is: Imitate the example and the virtues of Christ. 'Do and suffer what He did and suffered.' So also I Peter 2:21: 'Christ suffered for us leaving us an example, that we should follow in His steps.' In Christ we see the height of patience, gentleness and love, and an admirable moderation in all things. We ought to put on this adornment of Christ, that is, imitate these virtues of His. In this sense we can imitate other saints as well.

> But to put on Christ according to the Gospel is a matter, not of imitation but of ... the rebirth and renewal that takes place in Baptism .... Paul is speaking about a 'putting on,' not by imitation but by birth.[25]

Sacramentum et Exemplum

While Luther understood that Christ cannot be seen solely in terms of his exemplary function, he also recognized that Christ must not be perceived solely in terms of his expiatory function. For a faith rooted in an historical incarnation, to preach the cross event as *sacramentum* alone is to slip into spiritualism or intellectual abstraction. The danger is that ultimately Christ's sacrifice may be reduced to simply a formula or a slogan of merely symbolic validity and a rationale for a hidden self-justification. The *theologia crucis* without an emphasis on the need to experientially participate in the cross is itself transformed into a *theologia gloria*.

Luther understood that Christ's sacrificial death must be seen to include both the *sacramentum et exemplum* -- both what Christ has done *for* us and *before* us. The historical Jesus provides us with a prophetic example which, as Luther emphasizes again and again, exists in order to be imitated. "When we have put on Christ as the role of our righteousness and our salvation, then we must put on Christ also as the garment of imitation."[26] The proper response to the *sacramentum* of the suffering and humiliated Christ is faith, while the example of Christ "behooves us to imitate Him."[27]

- 2 -

In order to understand Luther's seemingly inconsistent attitude toward the imitation of Christ, it must be remembered that the late medieval understanding of the imitation of Christ had two components. The first component was the ethical/moral while the second was the theological/soteriological. For medieval piety, the moral life was the road leading to fellowship with God. The imitation of Christ resulted in a *conformitas voluntatis (et rationis) Dei*, culminating in righteousness and salvation.

It is clear, given Luther's many statements criticizing the *imitatio* motif, that he rejected much of its medieval formulation. Medieval piety, with its emphasis upon the attainment of *similitudo*, had made of the *imitatio Christi* a law, a precondition for the reception of grace and a methodological formula for salvation. In his development of *sola fide, sola gratia* as the central theological factors of his *conformitas Christi* position, Luther had come to reject entirely the meritorious or soteriological function of the imitation of Christ. The imitation of Christ cannot conform us to Christ. To do so would be to deny our true status as *peccator* and to deny our profound need for grace.

Luther's understanding does not begin with the works of humanity but with God's work of grace for humanity. By asserting the primacy of the *Christus sacramentum* over the *Christus exemplum*, Luther affirms a sequential order (but not in a temporal sense) which cannot be reversed. For example, again in his Hebrews commentary, Luther writes: "Whoever therefore, would imitate Christ as He is the *exemplum* must believe first with a firm faith that Christ suffered for him as *sacramentum*."[28]   Rather than viewing the imitation of Christ as conforming the Christian to the will of God, Luther rejected any ethical or moral imitation of the *Christus exemplum* unless and until one is first conformed to Christ by means of one's faith in the *Christus sacramentum*.

Due in part, no doubt, to his emphasis upon the *Christus sacramentum*, some theologians have largely ignored Luther's retention of the *Christus exemplum*. Lennart Pinomaa, for one, is certainly correct when he argues that, "Luther rejected the idea that Christ is primarily our example"; however, Pinomaa is incorrect in suggesting further that, according to Luther, Christians must choose "either *Christus exemplum* or *Christus sacramentum*." The historical evidence does not support this conclusion. According to Luther, the *Christus exemplum* is dependent upon Christ as *sacramentum*, but faith in Christ's sacrifice does not exclude the example of Christ. The imitation of Christ was understood by Luther as a corollary of grace, dependent and based upon faith in the prior work of Christ. Nevertheless, once grasped by grace and conformed to Christ, the faithful remain obliged to imitate Christ.

Sacramentum et Exemplum

Luther rejected medieval piety which placed the example of Christ before the *Christus sacramentum*, works before faith and the imitation of Christ before *conformitas Christi*, but he never rejected good works or the imitation of Christ. In fact, it is faith in Christ's sacrifice which in turn obliges or 'behooves' us to imitate and live according to the example of Christ. This reversal of the traditional medieval order, rather than the compulsion of an existential choice, is the truly revolutionary aspect of Luther's Christological and ethical thought.

There are several questions that remain to be answered. First of all, does the imitation of Christ, as outlined in the previous pages, remain as an ingredient of Luther's thought throughout his career or was it only in the so-called 'Catholic' Luther, dominated by Augustine's categories, that the imitation of Christ is to be found?[29] Secondly, if the imitation of Christ can be shown to be a continuous element of Luther's thought, what is its function and what are its parameters given Luther's rejection of any meritoriousness or soteriological significance? Finally, if the imitation of Christ can be shown to be a significant component of Luther's thought, why have Luther scholars generally failed to acknowledge it and even suggest, as has Pinomaa, that the imitation of Christ is incompatible with *sola fide*, *sola gratia* and that the *Christus sacramentum* is incompatible with the *Christus exemplum*? In order to answer these questions requires turning to the later stages of Luther's thought and specifically to his understanding of *sola fide* and its relationship to good works.

NOTES

1. Bernard, *On the Song of Songs*, XLIII.4.

2. For an examination of the *Christus sacramentum* in Augustine, see C. Couturier, "*Sacramentum et Mysterium* dans l'Oeuvre de Saint Augustin," *Études Augustiniennes*, 28 (1953), *passim*.

3. See Lohse, "Die Bedeutung Augustins für den jungen Luther," p. 133.

4. See Iserloh, *"Sacramentum et exemplum,* ein augustinisches Thema lutherischer Theologie," pp. 247-264.

5. See Norman Nagel, *"Sacramentum et Exemplum* in Luther's Understanding of Christ," in *Luther for an Ecumenical Age,* pp. 172-199.

6. "We were buried ... with him by baptism into death, so that as Christ was raised from the dead by the glory of the Father, we too might walk in newness of life" -- Romans 6:4 (RSV).

7. *WA* 56, p. 321.

8. *WA* 10 I, p. 10.

9. *WA* 57 III, p. 223. "Therefore, brethren, since we have confidence to enter the sanctuary by the blood of Jesus, by the new and living way which we opened for us through the curtain, that is, through his flesh, and since we have a great priest over the house of God, let us draw near with a true heart in full assurance of faith, with our hearts sprinkled clean from an evil conscience and our bodies washed with pure water" -- Hebrews 10:19-22 (RSV).

10. For an examination of Luther's Hebrews lectures and commentary emphasizing this transition of exegetical principles, see Kenneth Hagen, *A Theology of Testament in the Young Luther: The Lectures on Hebrews,* Vol. XII of the series *Studies in Medieval and Reformation Thought;* see also Darrell R. Reinke, "From Allegory to Metaphor: More Notes on Luther's Hermeneutical Shift," *Harvard Theological Review,* 66 (1973), pp. 386-395.

11. *WA* 57 III, p. 114; see also *WA* 9, pp. 18-19.

12. John Headley writes, "In Luther's judgment scholastic theology had curtailed the sacramental significance of Christ and had cultivated his exemplary significance" (*Luther's View of Church History,* p. 24); see also pp. 46-53.

13. Oberman, *Harvest of Medieval Theology,* p. 267.

14. See Hägglund, "The Background of Luther's Doctrine of Justification in Late Medieval Theology," pp. 31-33.

15. *WA* 2, p. 521, *LW* 27, p. 268; *WA* 40 I, p. 451, *LW* 26, p. 284; *WA* 40 I, p. 503, *LW* 26, p. 325.

16. See Anselm, *Cur deus homo?,* esp. Bk. I, pp. 11-21, and Bk. II, pp. 4-6, 11, 19-20. Reprinted in Eugene R. Fairweather, ed., *A Scholastic Miscellany:*

Anselm to Ockham, Vol. X of the series *The Library of Christian Classics* (Philadelphia: Westminster Press; London: SCM Press, 1956), pp. 101-102, 118-120, 135-139, 150-153, 163-164, 176, 180-181, 181-182, 183.

17. *WA* 31, p. 264.

18. *LW* 51, p. 92; *WA* 10 III, p. 49.

19. See Prenter, *Spiritus Creator*, p. 92.

20. See Heinrich Bornkamm, *Luther's World of Thought* (Saint Louis: Concordia Publishing House, 1958), pp. 93-114.

21. *WA* 57 III, p. 223.

22. See Pinomaa, *Faith Victorious*, p. 48.

23. Gustaf Wingren also argues, "Christ is not to be imitated by us, but rather to be accepted in faith" ("The Christian's Calling According to Luther," p. 172). Regin Prenter uses a similar argument when he writes, "The relationship to the historic Christ is not understood under the law as an imitation, but by the Gospel as a conformity, not as a result of the initiative of man, but as the result of the *opus alienum* and *proprium* of God who is present" (*Spiritus Creator*, pp. 25-26).

24. *WA* 2, p. 501; *LW* 27, p. 238; see also *WA* 57 III, p. 114.

25. *LW* 26, pp. 352-353; see also *LW* 35, pp. 119ff., *WA* 10 I, pp. 10ff., *LW* 27, p. 126.

26. *LW* 27, p. 128; see also *LW* 27, p. 34 and *WA* 57 III, p. 222.

27. *LW* 27, p. 238; *WA* 2, p. 501; see also *LW* 25, p. 309 and *LW* 35, p. 120.

28. *WA* 57 III, p. 114.

29. Norman Nagel argues that although Luther may have advocated the *sacramentum et exemplum* Christology during his early career, he was to reject it in his 'mature' theology. "To the extent that the *sacramentum et exemplum* put in an appearance ... they are like pterodactyles flying backwards. Luther could never leave well enough alone .... (W)hen he trots out his *sacramentum et exemplum* for disputation, pedagogically this may be excused. And in his Table Talk we cannot insist that he mind his P's and Q's" ("*Sacramentum et Exemplum* in Luther's Understanding of Christ," p. 175; see also pp. 183, 188 *et passim*).

Despite Nagel's warning, the many references to the *sacramentum et exemplum* in Luther's later writings cannot be ignored. For example, in thesis 50 of his first *Disputation Against the Antinomians* (1538) Luther writes, "We know, and they have learned from us, that Christ became both sacrament and example for us" (*WA* 39 I, p. 356). In his second *Disputation* Luther reaffirms this complementariness. "You know that Paul usually joins two things, just as Peter did in First Peter 2:21; first that Christ died for us and redeemed us through His blood to purify for Himself a Holy people. Thus he shows us Christ as gift and sacrament. Then, they show us Christ as an example we should imitate in His good works" (*WA* 39 I, p. 462).

Nagel claims that references from Luther's disputations and 'table-talk' are not credible. However, there are many other references in his Biblical commentaries which were not written in the heat of dispute and reveal a well-reasoned approach (see *LW* 26, pp. 352ff.). Erwin Iserloh, commenting on the *sacramentum et exemplum* writes, "This pair of concepts and the underlying idea turn up not just in Luther's early works, where they might be written off as results of his study of Augustine, but as well through the whole work of the Reformer. The formula is especially amazing when one's idea of Luther's doctrine has been too much influenced by the systematization of Lutheran orthodoxy and by the textbooks stemming from that tradition" ("Luther's Christ-Mysticism," p. 54; see also pp. 37-58).

VI. GOOD WORKS

A. *Sola Fide* and Good Works

- 1 -

Luther originally came to public attention as a result of his objections to the selling of indulgences in the Archbishopric of Mainz by Johann Tetzel (c. 1465-1519).[1] Although the sale of indulgences was the specific issue Luther addressed in his *Ninety-Five Theses*, this in itself was not the basis of his controversy with the Church. After all, Luther was not the first to object to the practice.[2] Reform was occurring throughout the Church. Tetzel's practices were clearly a malpractice of the original teaching on indulgences, and if it were not for the self-interest and intransigence of Luther's superiors, the issue could likely have been settled.

Within a church in which the religious life and lay piety were so dominated by rites and practices intended to placate God and place one on the side of the angels, good works were the *conditio sine qua non* of a saving grace. Luther had already questioned and shown his dissatisfaction with a theology which asserted that good works permitted the Christian to cooperate with God in the attainment of salvation. As a result the door had been opened for Luther's criticism of the entire range of works and penitential practices which were claimed to have a meritorious and soteriological significance. While some reformers were attempting to restrict the claims and sales of indulgences, Luther rejected them entirely. What Luther wanted was not simply the reform of certain practices, but their abolition. It was not only the practices, but the underlying teachings themselves, that were at fault.

Luther believed that what were traditionally accepted as good works, such as the practice of celibacy, the observation of feast days, fasting and the like, were merely acts of appeasement and self-righteous attempts at self-salvation. Luther recognized the depth of corruption of the self which attempts to turn all goods to itself. The extraordinary affectations of asceticism are ultimately designed to serve the self amidst claims to self-denial. Luther responded that good works are never those which are done to appease God. In fact, it is impossible to pacify God. Penitential practices, therefore, should not even be classified as good works, for their intent is to appease God and their basic motivation is to serve the self.

Luther's development of *sola fide, sola gratia* as the basis of the Christian life did not entail a wholesale denial of good works but only their efficaciousness *coram Deo*. Luther's rejection of certain practices generally regarded as good works, and his criticism of the self-centred motivation provided by the *actum meritorium* soteriological framework of scholastic theology, point to a radically new definition of what constitutes a good work. Luther writes: "Those actions we do in relationship to God are not called good works, but what we do for our neighbour, those are good works."[3] And further: "God having no need of our works and benefactions for Himself bids us do for our neighbour what we would do for God."[4]

If good works are understood as neighbour-centred, then it is the neighbour who will become the true beneficiary of our works. If works are done for the sake of God, then within those works may be seen a hidden agenda for merit and salvation. To do good works for the sake of God presumptuously assumes that God has need of our works. To do good works for the sake of merit and salvation ultimately reduces the neighbour to the status of a stumbling block to salvation. Luther, on the other hand, affirmed the all-sufficiency of God, arguing

Good Works

that God "does not need our efforts but our neighbour has need of our deeds."[5] Put simply, to do good works for God, we attempt to serve ourselves, whereas to do good works for our neighbour, we truly serve God.[6]

- 2 -

Luther regarded performing good works for the sake of merit, appeasement and salvation as little more than "a bridge and stairway of spider webs."[7] Nevertheless he did not reject good works. While Luther argued that salvation is a free gift to be humbly accepted in faith, he did not preclude the obligation of Christians to do good works. "(F)aith and good works must be held together," writes Luther, "so that in both the Christian life is contained."[8]

Although emphasizing that faith and good works 'must be held together,' Luther often deals with them independently, as he did with the two essentially interrelated aspects of his Christology -- the *sacramentum et exemplum*. In his view, both had been misunderstood in their theological status within the Christian ethos. Not only do faith and works have to be understood anew, but they must also be reinterpreted in terms of their relationship to each other. Just as the *Christus sacramentum* has precedence over the example of Christ, and *conformitas Christi* primacy over the imitation of Christ, Luther maintains that the relationship between faith and works must also be seen in a distinct, sequential order. For Luther, "Faith is the beginning (first principle) of all good works."[9]

Luther often spoke in terms of this sequential ordering of faith and works, faith belonging to heaven and works to the world, or the true following of Christ in faith and a secondary following of works. In his Heidelberg Disputation of 1518, Luther explains the significance of faith in the work of Christ for our own works.

> Since Christ lives in us through faith, so He arouses us to do good works through the living faith in His work, for the works which He does are the fulfilment of the commands of God given us through

faith. If we look at them we are moved to imitate them. For this reason the Apostle says, 'Therefore be imitators of God, as beloved children' (Eph. 5:1). Thus deeds of mercy are aroused by the works through which He has saved us, as St. Gregory says: Every act of Christ is instruction for us, indeed, a stimulant.[10]

It is not our work, but God's works of grace in Christ which is primary. Our works are acceptable to God only because of the sacrifice of Christ. Moreover, faith in Christ also provides the *potentia* or impetus and power to perform works. We are aroused and motivated by the works through which he has saved us. The *Christus exemplum*, understood in light of faith, provides a 'stimulant' which 'we are moved to imitate.' Clearly the imitation of Christ cannot be the decisive event in the Christian life. As Luther makes clear, it is a corollary which, although providing exemplary guidance and 'instruction,' is contingent upon faith in the primary work of the *Christus sacramentum*.

B. Christology and Good Works

- 1 -

It must be reiterated that when Luther speaks of performing good works in imitation of Christ, he does not attribute any meritorious or soteriological significance to these works. The imitation of Christ must never be understood as a basis for an exchange of properties (e.g., righteousness) or for fellowship with Christ. It must also be remembered that in advocating the imitation of Christ, Luther is not speaking in terms of the imitation of specific works. Earlier in his career Luther made the important distinction between the *imitatio operis* and the *imitatio mentis*. It remains clear that when Luther advocates the imitation of Christ he is emphasizing the imitation of revealed attitudes, intentions and motivations which shaped the life of Christ rather than specific works. Over the years, Luther's understanding of these essential motifs, which he believed characterized Christ's life, also underwent a significant transformation.

Prior to his development of *sola fide, sola gratia,* the characteristic motif of Luther's imitation of Christ, as originally derived from Stapulensis and the penitential *theologia crucis* tradition, had been to resign oneself to suffering. At a later date, this motif was slightly modified by Luther. He concluded that a humble faith in the midst of bearing the cross imitates Christ 'in a proper sense.' Both instances, nonetheless, were largely personal, internal and rather passive conceptions of the life of faith and did not speak of the Christian life *coram hominibus.* Luther's full development of justification by grace through faith and consequent redefinition of good works entailed a reinterpretation of the Christian life as informed by the example of Christ.

In Philippians 2:5-7, Luther read of Christ taking the form of a servant *(forma servii).*[11] In his exegesis, Luther writes: "This is a truly Christian life. Here faith is truly active through love."[12] In the life and death of Christ, Luther saw the active life of faith expressed through works of love toward our neighbour.[13] This must be the characteristic form of the Christian life as well. Luther writes: "(E)ach individual Christian shall become the servant of another in accordance with the example of Christ."[14] 'Faith active through love' imitates Christ 'in a proper sense.'

This is not to suggest that 'faith active through love' supplanted 'faith in the midst of bearing the cross' as the essence of Luther's understanding of the imitation of Christ. For Luther, Christ's works and his sacrificial death on the cross were both examples of love for humanity. Both were gifts. Both were expressions of the *Christus pro nobis* to be humbly accepted in faith. It would be more accurate to state that 'faith active through love' supplemented rather than supplanted 'faith in the midst of bearing the cross' as the characteristic motifs of the Christian life as exemplified in the life and death of Christ.

- 2 -

While advocating that we perform good works in imitation of Christ, Luther was always certain to remind us that "we must beware that the active life with its works ... (does) not lead us astray."[15] The imitation of Christ can never do more than provide guidance for us in our relationships with our neighbours, as opposed to medieval theology in which the imitation of Christ served as a methodological formula or a pathway to salvation. When salvation is seen as Calvary-centred, the imitation of Christ loses any salvific function. Faith in the *Christus sacramentum* has to do with our relationship to God, while the imitation of Christ has to do solely with our relationship to our neighbour.

The imitation of Christ, in providing normative guidance for the moral life, is merely a description or symbol of the life demanded of Christians. It does not have within itself the potential to achieve that toward which it strives. The works we do, even if performed in imitation of Christ, can never in themselves be considered as 'good' and are unacceptable to God.

The imitation of Christ does not make us 'like' Christ. Christ alone was without sin. Only through the communion of faith can we be granted the righteousness that Christ exemplified in his life. Only Christ's substitutionary sacrifice and our faith in the *Christus sacramentum* can make our works 'good' and acceptable to God.

Christ is the gift of faith whose sacrifice provided us with an example of a truly Christian life.

> Christ is yours, presented to you as a gift. After that it is necessary that you turn this into an example and deal with your neighbour in the very same way, be given also to him as a gift and an example .... This double kindness is the twofold aspect of Christ; gift and example.[16]

The fact that Christ is given to us as a gift should in itself be an example for us. As Christ is a gift to us, we also ought to be a gift to others. As Christ is an example to us, we also ought to be an example to others. As Christ has

111

suffered for us, we should be willing to suffer for others. As Christ carried our cross for us, we should be willing to carry the neighbour's cross. We must "become a Christ to (our) neighbour and be for him what Christ is for me."[17]

We are to love our neighbour -- not for the sake of merit, not with the mistaken notion that we will thereby be saved, not for our own sake -- but solely for the sake of our neighbour, in accordance with the example of Christ. We are to serve the needs of the *proximus*, enemy as well as friend -- not in order to transmute their enmity to friendship, not for the sake of enlightened self-interest -- but as Christ served us.

> I will therefore give myself as a Christ to my neighbour, just as Christ offered Himself to me; I will do nothing in this life except what I see as necessary, profitable, and salutary to my neighbour, since through faith I have an abundance of all good things in Christ.[18]

Love for the neighbour expressed through good works has become the consequence of one's faith, rather than a means of attaining or cooperating in the attainment of salvation. The *imitatio Christi*, purged of its alliance to efficaciousness and meritoriousness, righteousness and soteriology, was now able to become the leitmotif of the moral life with the example of Christ providing guidance for our works.

C. *Treatise on Good Works*

- 1 -

During the developing controversy with the Roman Church, Luther continued to be strongly critical of the late medieval understanding of the *Christus exemplum, imitatio Christi* and good works, associated as they were with claims of righteousness, meritoriousness and soteriology. He thereby oftentimes obscured the positive regard he had for them. In 1520, Luther's old friend, Georg Spalatin (1484-1545), a member of the Erfurt circle of reform-minded Erasmian humanists, urged Luther to prepare a sermon on the subject of faith and good works. According to Spalatin, Luther's stress on *sola fides justificat* was reported to have led to a neglect of good works and a rise in lawlessness, immorality and even revolt among some of his followers who, nevertheless, felt justified in their actions.[19]

The role of good works in Luther's thought had been misunderstood, a confusion which can be attributed, in large part, to Luther himself. However, Luther tended to place the blame for the unfortunate consequences of his teaching on the moral laxity of his followers. Luther writes:

> (I)f grace or faith is not preached, no one is saved; for faith alone justifies and saves. On the other hand, if faith is preached ... the majority of men understand the teaching about faith in a fleshly way and transform the freedom of the Spirit into the freedom of the flesh.[20]

Luther's sermon was to grow into his *Treatise on Good Works* (1520). Still embroiled in his disputations with the Roman Church over indulgences and penitential practices, works-righteousness and meritoriousness, Luther continues to be concerned primarily with the defense of *sola fide, sola gratia*. Luther reaffirms his thesis, namely that justification by grace through faith is the sole basis and source of the moral life and its good works. Christians are justified solely by their faith, and God's grace is such that Christians are absolutely free of the requirement of performing works in order to be 'reckoned unto righteousness.' Quite simply, a work is good if done by one who is justified whatever the work may ultimately be, and evil if not done on this basis. Good or evil works are only definable as such by the presence or absence of justification by grace through faith in the agent. "(E)veryone who lacks faith sins, even if he acts well."[21] Right relationship to God alone determines the 'goodness' of a work.[22]

Removing good works from their association with meritoriousness aided Luther in undermining the prevalent belief of medieval piety in a dichotomy of works, which claimed that a distinction exists in God's sight between the 'superior' works of the clerics and the 'inferior' or secular works of the laity. An ethos which holds that one must first perform works in order to obtain God's approval is ultimately compelled to find special 'pious' or 'holy' works different from ordinary good works. To this Luther responds that there are no good works except those done in faith, and by this faith all works are made alike. Luther writes: "Let all our works be good whatever they may be, without any distinction. And they are (good) when I am certain and believe that they please God."[23]

The radical nature of Luther's understanding of *sola fide, sola gratia* frees the doctrine of works from any hierarchy of values in which some works are seen as of greater value than others. In light of faith, all works have equal value -- none have greater value *coram Deo* than others. There are, of course, distinctions within the realm of works. These are, however, always relativized in relation to faith.

- 2 -

In spite of, or perhaps due to, his critique of works-righteousness, there were few who wrote more about good works than did Luther. It was incumbent upon Luther, in his *Treatise on Good Works*, to restate his doctrine of faith and works in such a way that it could not be misused by his own followers, some of whom felt that in light of *sola fide, sola gratia* it was no longer necessary to perform works. Indeed, if there is no need or requirement to perform works in order to be 'reckoned unto righteousness,' and if faith is all that is necessary, then why must good works be done at all?

However, in the face of continuing criticism by the Roman forces which opposed him, Luther did not address these concerns. He had become so careful to stress the primacy of *sola fide, sola gratia* and the prior work of the *Christus sacramentum*, and careful also to disassociate good works from meritoriousness so that a doctrine of good works would not lead the faithful to self-reliance and pride, that the significance of good works appears to have become depreciated in his thought. Luther's use of polemics in his continuing defense of *sola fide, sola gratia* tended to return the one-sidedness of the attack against him by his own one-sidedness.

While Luther's use of polemics and paradox placed grace and faith in the centre of what it meant to be a Christian, the resulting theological edifice created by Luther was seen by some reformers as having failed to sustain the simple piety or lead to the social changes that many of them sought. Luther's belief that "(w)orks issue spontaneously from faith,"[24] with the seemingly inherent optimism of a natural spontaneity or disposition reminiscent of the *facere quod in se est*, had not laid the issue of good works to rest. The role and status of good works and their relationship to the imitation of Christ and the *Christus exemplum*, which he did not adequately address in his treatise, remained issues Luther was to be continuously confronted with -- and from this time on, not only by Roman Catholics but also by representatives of the forces he himself had helped to unleash.

NOTES

1. Indulgences were originally introduced so that merit could be accrued on the basis of financial contribution for those who could not go on the Crusades. Soon indulgences became so lucrative that they remitted not only penalties imposed by the Church, but also forgave sins of the past, present and future and were applicable even to Purgatory. See Ozment, "Luther and the Late Middle Ages: The Formation of Reformation Thought," pp. 109-129.

2. Jean Gerson more than a century earlier had also opposed the sale of indulgences, as did Johannes Rucherath von Oberwessel (d. 1481), known as Johannes von Wessel, Ockhamist Rector of the University of Erfurt (c. 1457). Von Wessel was condemned by the Inquisition (1479) for his support of the Hussites and criticism of the Church's practice of the distribution of the merits of the saints by means of indulgences (Iserloh, "Theology in the Age of

Transition," *Handbook of Church History*, IV, pp. 595-597). Among Luther's contemporaries, many Humanists also rejected the sale of indulgences (Roland Bainton, *Here I Stand: A Life of Martin Luther* (New York: Pierce and Smith, 1950), p. 96).

3. *WA* 10 III, p. 98.

4. *WA* 17, p. 98.

5. *WA* 25, p. 394.

6. We must be careful at this point not to separate the two aspects of our relationship to God and neighbour. Insofar as works are done out of faith, even if intended for the neighbour, they are still of value to God. "Every work of a Christian shall be a service to God" (*WA* 4, p. 653).

7. *WA* 45, p. 493.

8. *WA* 12, p. 289.

9. *WA* 5, p. 119.

10. *LW* 31, pp. 56-57.

11. *LW* 31, p. 301, *LW* 31, p. 303. "Have this mind among yourselves, which you have in Christ Jesus, who, though he was in the form of God, did not count equality with God a thing to be grasped, but emptied himself, taking the form of a servant (slave), being born in the likeness of man" -- Philippians 2:5-7 (RSV).

12. *LW* 31, p. 365.

13. See George Forrell, *Faith Active in Love* (Minneapolis: Augsburg, 1959), *passim*; cf. Donald C. Ziemke, *Love for the Neighbor in Luther's Theology: The Development of His Thought, 1512-1529* (Minneapolis: Augsburg, 1963), *passim*.

14. *LW* 31, p. 302; see also *LW* 35, p. 120.

15. *WA* 5, p. 84.

16. *LW* 35, p. 121; see also *WA* 33, p. 522. Luther sometimes refers to Christ's sacrifice as both gift and example while at other times simply as gift. Similarly Luther sometimes refers to Christ solely as gift while at other times as both gift and example. Luther was inconsistent in this regard, leaving no clear indication of which formulation he preferred.

17. *WA* 7, p. 35; see also *LW* 31, pp. 300ff. Roland Bainton has characterized Luther's phrase 'become a Christ to the neighbour' as "the epitome of Luther's ethic." Bainton asks rhetorically, "Where will one find a nobler restoration of ethics, and where will one find anything more devastating to ethics?" (*Here I Stand*, p. 179). And elsewhere, "The essence of Christian morality (for Luther), is the imitation of Christ, not in the medieval sense of doing just what Christ did but rather in behaving after the pattern of Christ" (*The Reformation of the 16th Century*, p. 52). See also Martin E. Marty, "Luther on Ethics: Man Free and Slave," in *Accents in Luther's Theology: Essays in Commemoration of the 450th Anniversary of the Reformation*, ed. H. O. Kadai (Saint Louis: Concordia, 1967), pp. 199-227.

18. *WA* 7, p. 66; *LW* 31, p. 367.

19. *WA* 6, p. 196.

20. *LW* 27, p. 48; *WA* 40 II, p. 60.

21. *WA* 56, p. 113.

22. See Paul Althaus, *The Ethics of Martin Luther* (Philadelphia: Fortress Press, 1962), esp. pp. 3-19.

23. *LW* 44, pp. 24-25.

24. *WA* 57 III, p. 114; see also *LW* 27, p. 96; *WA* 40 II, p. 121.

VII. LUTHER AND KARLSTADT

A. Luther and Karlstadt on the Spirit of Reform

- 1 -

In 1521-22, while Luther was in seclusion in the Wartburg, engaged with the translation of Erasmus' Greek text of the New Testament into German, the leadership of the reform movement in Wittenberg fell to his old friends and colleagues, Philipp Melanchthon (1497-1560) and Andreas Bodenstein von Karlstadt (c. 1480-1541). Karlstadt, the former professor and Dean of the University of Wittenberg (1505-1522), had been the senior debator with Luther at the Heidelberg (1518) and Leipzig (1519) disputations.[1]

Karlstadt, originally a Thomist, was more cautious than Luther in his comments on indulgences and his challenge to Papal authority. Karlstadt believed that change would take place within the Wittenberg magisterial system if one proceeded cautiously. Believing Melanchthon was becoming too radicalized by his desire for change, Karlstadt argued that change must come, "by all means, but without tumult and without giving opponents an opportunity for slander."[2]

After his excommunication, and with all the zeal of a new convert, Karlstadt became determined to carry out a concrete renovation of the ecclesiastical order. He turned his attention from theological debate to practical religious reform, celebrating the first Protestant communion on Christmas Day of 1521. He soon attempted to implement other ecclesiastical and even social reforms -- moreover, in the face of princely objection if this proved to be necessary.

Peasant insurrections against the financial holdings of the Roman Church had been frequent throughout the fifteenth and sixteenth centuries. The peasants believed that now the Church could be safely overthrown without the forfeit of spiritual benefits. Although the princes had a vested political and economic interest in seeing the reformation succeed, they feared that the murder of monks would invite Roman intervention. After all, the armies of Charles V were poised only a few kilometres away in Vienna defending the Empire against Islamic expansion. Together with Gabriel Zwilling and Nicholas Storch, the leader of the Zwickau prophets, Karlstadt was blamed for fomenting the Wittenberg riots of 1522.

- 2 -

After his return to Wittenberg, Martin Luther saw as his primary duty the building and preservation of a new church. He came to believe that this church would be able to take root only in those regions where it had the support of the ruling princes. Luther was made aware that the threat of rebellion and insurrection would lose him this much-needed support of the princes. He soon came to regard Karlstadt and the unchecked spirit for radical reform as the greatest obstacles to the survival of the reformation.

In his *Sincere Admonition to All Christians to Guard Against Insurrection and Rebellion* (1522), Luther argued that insurrection, in its indiscriminate use of violence aimed at the Roman Church, was not necessary to destroy clerical power, for "Christ Himself had already begun an insurrection with His mouth, one which will be more than the Pope can bear."[3] Luther argued that clerical power "will not be destroyed by the hand of men, but by the wrath of God itself, *without any intermediary*."[4] For Luther, faith required an unconditional trust in the unaided power of the Word. He pleaded that the only weapon used be the Gospel alone for a trial period of two more years as it had been during the past year in which so much had been accomplished.

While he turned his voice of moderation to the peasants, Luther's anger became focused on his old friend and ally. Karlstadt was severely criticized by Luther and his theology dismissed largely because of his politics. In his *Against the Heavenly Prophets* (1525) Luther writes, "One can believe no one who ... storms against God's accustomed order."[5] Although Luther had himself technically lived in a state of civil disobedience since 1521, ironically he now criticized Karlstadt for 'running counter' to "the power and might of the reigning prince and the governing authority which God has initiated."[6] Karlstadt was ridiculed for not remaining in his proper station within the University and for trading in his Doctor's gown for peasant's garb. Karlstadt, who had conferred the degree of Doctor on Luther, now rejected his own. Luther responded angrily:

> What think you now? Is it not a fine new spiritual humility? Wearing a felt hat and gray garb, not wanting to be called Doctor, but Brother Andrew and dear neighbour as another peasant .... (By) this self-chosen humility and servility, which God does not command, he (Karlstadt) wanted to be seen and praised as a remarkable Christian, as though Christian behaviour consisted in such external hocus-pocus.[7]

- 3 -

Luther's belief that in light of faith all works are alike informed his understanding of the 'priesthood of all believers' and ultimately the secular vocation (*Beruf*).[8] For Luther, one's vocation was to be practised within the 'stations' (*Standorte*) in life in which one found oneself. With one's 'office' (*Amt*) within a station come certain duties and responsibilities (*Befehl*). We receive our personal calling through the recognition of the particular demands inherent within the stations, whether marriage and family or the *status economicus, politicus* or *ecclesiasticus*. These stations are seen by Luther as objective orders or categories of human interaction and relationship which preserve humanity and establish order, justice and peace in the world.[9] Rebellion against the order, justice and peace provided by the stations is rebellion against God and will "bring down judgment upon yourself, and the stone thrown upward toward heaven will fall on your head."[10] In keeping with most late medieval thought, Luther held that the fixed and rigid social order was a reflection of the God-created cosmic order.[11]

Although his 'priesthood of all believers' had radical theological and ecclesiastical ramifications, Luther's understanding of *Beruf* retained a basically conservative medieval political view of social stratification and mobility. In fact, it can be argued that Luther's doctrine of *Beruf*, in adding theological sanctification to the static nature of the stations, in itself helped to maintain the prevalent medieval economic and political order against the onslaught of other social forces that had been unleashed.

B. Luther and Karlstadt on Faith, Christology and Good Works

- 1 -

In response to the call for social reform, Luther appears to retreat from his 'faith active through love' position -- a position which would tend to support social activism -- returning to his roots in Germanic mystical theology with his 'faith in the midst of bearing the cross' position of earlier years. Luther's *theologia crucis* was, however, basically a passive stance and it is this element which again comes to the fore. In his *Admonition to Peace* (1525) Luther writes:

> The Gospel does not become involved in the affairs of this world,
> but speaks of our life in the world in terms of suffering and

injustice, the cross, patience and contempt for this life and temporal wealth.[12]

Luther clearly never intended his theology to provide the basis for economic, political or social reform. The Kingdom cannot be erected on earth. The life of faith, as now emphasized by Luther, was to entail the passive acceptance of the given social order, which in itself is God's gift to humanity, and through which God bestows other gifts upon humanity.

While advocating a *theologia crucis* for others, it did not occur to Luther that his own position had much in common with a *theologia gloria*. Luther was not passive in the face of social forces. His fear of chaos and need to preserve the reformation drove him to side with the power and might of the princes.

Karlstadt and the so-called left-wing of the reformation had increasingly divergent conceptions of Christian conduct from that of Luther.[13] Karlstadt wanted not only right doctrine, as did Luther, but also a significant place for good works, which he correctly felt Luther was becoming less and less concerned with. Karlstadt writes:

> Accursed and abominable before God is he who is lazy in bursting forth with works for the betterment of his neighbour. God wants a completely willing giver, one who gives quickly and voluntarily. A ready, willing mind inclined to action pleases God (II Cor. 9:7) .... He who remembers divine teaching properly and well cannot stand still or be idle or peevish when God's sayings obligate and impel him to action. If he holds still in a situation where he can and should work, that is a certain sign that he had forgotten or does not have the kind of remembrance that he should have, that is, from his whole heart (Deut. 29).[14]

For Karlstadt, post-conversion Christian conduct demanded a significant change in lifestyles, as witnessed by an active imitation of Christ as revealed in the Gospels. *Beruf* was redefined by Karlstadt with a greater emphasis upon a life of active discipleship which demanded good works in a larger societal sense than acts of love within interpersonal relationships as Luther was advocating. Karlstadt simply wanted to concretize and bring to fruition what he considered were the social implications of *sola fides justificat* and the imitation of Christ. It was from this perspective that Karlstadt accuses Luther of preaching only 'the sweet Christ' and a faith not requiring works, which he criticized and ultimately rejected as 'a phoney faith.'

- 2 -

Questions of the status of good works, the significance of the imitation of Christ and the role of the *Christus exemplum* had again become central issues. Karlstadt's insistence on the necessity of works made Luther suspect that he was attempting to link works to some manner of works-righteousness and meritoriousness and was reviving the scholastics' assertion of a soteriological significance for works. Luther accused Karlstadt of reducing Christology to the exemplary function of Christ alone. "Doctor Karlstadt's theology," writes Luther, "has not gotten beyond teaching how we are to imitate Christ, making of Christ only an example and a law-giver. From this only works can be learned."[15] Luther always emphasized that Christians who do not wish to go astray "must look beyond works, and beyond laws and doctrines about works."[16]

Clearly, as far as Karlstadt was concerned, this was not the issue. During this initial period of their dispute (c. 1521-1525), Karlstadt's position, as that of Luther, included both a *conformitas Christi* and the imitation of Christ.[17] Karlstadt writes that "We must be completely conformed to Christ (*Christformig*) *and* imitate Christ."[18]

In response, Luther accuses Karlstadt of returning to the medieval methodological formulation in which the imitation of Christ resulted in a *conformitas Christi*. According to Luther, Karlstadt "does not understand how Christ is first of all our salvation, and thereafter his works with the Word are our example."[19] Luther accuses Karlstadt of trying to 'reverse the orders of God,' claiming that "Dr. Karlstadt and his spirits replace the highest with the lowest, the best with the least, the first with the last."[20] And further, "No one can mortify the flesh, bear the cross and follow the example of Christ before he is a

Christian"[21] -- meaning before one is conformed to Christ and justified by grace through faith. "Whoever wants to propose to you another order, you can be sure is of the Devil."[22]

Again, clearly this was not the case. Affirming the same *ordo salutis* as Luther, in his *Review of Some of the Chief Articles of Christian Doctrine in which Dr. Luther brings Andreas Karlstadt under Suspicion through False Accusation and Calumny* (1525), Karlstadt writes:

> He who knows Christ has become free through the knowledge of Christ; and he walks in the works of Christ. But he does not become a Christian through works, just as one does not become a Christian through humble service, good deeds, help or financial assistance, etc.[23]

Despite the obvious similarities noted above, important differences between Luther and Karlstadt concerning issues of sin and soteriology and the role of the Spirit do exist and should not be minimized.[24] However, the differences concerning the relationship between *conformitas Christi* and the imitation of Christ, the role of the *Christus exemplum* and the status of works are not as readily apparent as Luther would have us believe. Although the particular role and political ramifications of their respective understanding of good works are markedly different, the differences between Luther and Karlstadt in terms of the theological status and nature of works are not so much a matter of theological substance but arose largely out of differences in political ideologies, temperament and emphasis. The differences are only secondarily and subsequently of a theological character.[25]

For example, while Luther argues that 'works follow faith', Karlstadt argues that, "Through the lack of such works, however, one would demonstrate that he is imprisoned in his heart ... and would attest that he had not yet become free in the truth."[26] For Luther, 'works issue spontaneously from faith,' while for Karlstadt, 'faith must lead to good works.' For Luther 'the good tree bears good fruits,' while for Karlstadt, 'the good fruits attest to the goodness of the tree.' For neither Luther nor Karlstadt does one become a Christian through works. Through the lack of works, however, Karlstadt believes that one cannot even be considered a true Christian. The differences in regard to good works are primarily a matter of the degree of emphasis concerning the non-soteriological requirement, obligation or necessity on the part of the Christian to perform works.

- 3 -

Both Luther and Karlstadt originally shared a common theological basis in that for both, faith in Christ or *conformitas Christi* 'behooves' the Christian to do good works in imitation of Christ. However, Luther's continuing struggle with the 'works-righteous' provided a continuing need to defend *sola fide, sola gratia* against those who he felt were forcing the reformation "to turn from the great important articles to minor ones."[27] Due to his tendency to ignore the consequential and evidential function of works, Luther's doctrine of faith appears increasingly removed from its relationship to works. Whenever challenged, Luther returns to his more passive and internal conception of the life of faith, and from that perspective quickly admonishes those who do otherwise, accusing them of works-righteousness. "They (the works-righteous) rush in to imitate the work of some great man or other. They rather ought to learn to keep silence before God and to have faith in God."[28]

Karlstadt did not keep silent. Responding to Luther's charge that the important articles were being ignored, Karlstadt writes:

> It means nothing that Luther alleges the chief articles are ignored and forgotten when we do battle over the other (articles). For there were and also still are other preachers and writers who preach and write while we deal with other points. Even if Dr. Luther and I slept, Dr. Luther need not worry, for the world does not depend on us.[29]

Even after his writings were banned by the Wittenberg censors, Karlstadt did not feel obliged "to refrain either in teaching or activity from carrying out God's commands until our neighbours and the guzzlers at Wittenberg followed."[30]

Luther and Karlstadt

Karlstadt continued to pursue the political goals of his active faith, criticizing "the sluggish and lazy brethren who sometimes purposely remain blind and lazy."[31] He was later linked to another radical movement led by the former Saxon Priest, Thomas Müntzer (c. 1490-1525). This complicity placed his life in danger. Luther met with Karlstadt in Jena to provide him with the opportunity to defend himself.[32]

Luther was apparently convinced by Karlstadt that he was not perverting doctrine, but after visiting Karlstadt's parish in Orlamünde, Luther came to question the sincerity of his disclaimer. Eventually he acquiesced to the princes' wish to have Karlstadt banished. The two Wittenberg reformers went their separate ways. Karlstadt left Saxony echoing Luther's own words after Worms, that he had been condemned "unheard and unconvicted."[33]

After his expulsion from Saxony, Karlstadt went to southern Germany. Shortly thereafter, Luther received correspondence from his ministers in Strassburg, the asylum for disaffected Lutherans and 'city of hope' for the radical reformation.

> We are not yet persuaded by Karlstadt but many of his arguments
> are weighty. We are disturbed because you have driven out your
> colleague with such inhumanity. At Basel and Zürich are many
> who agree with him.[34]

Karlstadt's expulsion did not lay to rest the questions of other reform groups concerning Luther's *sola fide, sola gratia*, the role of good works, the function of the imitation of Christ or the form of the *Christus exemplum*. Karlstadt's influence spread throughout southern Germany, finding a fertile ground among other sectarian Protestant groups who, for a variety of theological reasons, came to positions similar to that of Karlstadt. In terms of the issues of faith, grace and works and the imitation of Christ, which have been the focus of our concern, undoubtedly the most significant dispute was between Luther and the Anabaptists.[35]

126

NOTES

1. Von Staupitz sent Luther to accompany Karlstadt to Heidelberg. John Eck challenged Karlstadt, not Luther, to the Leipzig debate. The bull of excommunication of 1520 included both Karlstadt and Luther.

2. Karlstadt, as reprinted in *Karlstadt's Battle with Luther: Documents in a Liberal-Radical Debate*, ed. Ronald J. Sider (Philadelphia: Fortress Press, 1978), p. 148.

3. *LW* 45, p. 68.

4. *Ibid.*, p. 61 (italics mine).

5. *WA* 18, p. 96; *LW* 40, p. 113.

6. *LW* 40, p. 117.

7. *Ibid.*

8. Luther's understanding of *Beruf* is derived in large part from Johannes Tauler and the Germanic mystical tradition's understanding of *vocatio*. As if foreshadowing Luther's concept of *Beruf*, Tauler wrote that, "If I were not a priest I would consider it a great thing to be able to make shoes and I would like to make them better than anything else" (as quoted by Hoffman, *Luther and the Mystics*, p. 41; see also Iserloh, "The German Mystics," *Handbook of Church History*, IV, pp. 382ff.). This particular tradition of *vocatio*, which suggested that it was not necessary to be a cleric in order to be a true Christian, informed Luther's understanding of the 'priesthood of all believers' and ultimately his understanding of the secular vocation. Unlike Tauler (and incidentally Karlstadt as well), Luther did not believe in the superiority of one vocation over another. Positions of power such as prince, magistrate and soldier were not by nature less spiritually significant than the humble occupations of shoemaker or peasant.

Whereas prior to 1522 Luther understood *Beruf* in the open-ended sense of vocation or calling, in light of his dispute with Karlstadt, he now added the limiting qualifier of 'within the stations' in which one lives. While Luther argued that one's calling is fulfilled within the stations, Calvin was to argue later that it is fulfilled by or through the worldly stations. Had Luther not been faced with what he considered as an abuse of the doctrine of vocation by Karlstadt, one could speculate that he would have retained his original formulation which had more in common with that of Calvin.

For additonal information on Luther's understanding of *Beruf*, see Wingren, *Luther on Vocation, passim*; and Althaus, *The Ethics of Martin Luther*, pp. 36-42; and Wingren, "The Christian's Calling According to Luther," pp. 3-16.

9. See Martin Heinecken, "Luther and the 'Orders of Creation' in Relation to a Doctrine of Work and Vocation," *Lutheran Quarterly*, 4 (1952), pp. 393-414.

10. *LW* 45, p. 66.

11. Luther's conservatism regarding the stations may also be traced to the influence of Tauler. Tauler wrote, "One can, and should remain in the class in which he has been placed by God" (as quoted by Williams, "German Mysticism in the Polarization of Ethical Behaviour," p. 281). Nevertheless, the stations are not seen as entirely static by Luther. Laws may change, political regimes may change and even the Church can change, but the stations themselves "must remain if the world is to stand" (*LW* 13, p. 358; *WA* 31 I, p. 410). There was only one criterion -- the stations must "serve God and the world" (*LW* 46, p. 252; *WA* 30 II, p. 578).

12. *LW* 46, p. 35.

13. G. H. Williams points out that, for Luther, "The believer should imitate the suffering Christ, as it were, within his God-assigned role in ordered law-based society, and inwardly without the sectarian show of piety and disruption of orderly life in church, society or university." And elsewhere, "Luther's opponents in contrast, increasingly emphasized the suffering imitation of Christ, to which Luther gave ever less attention in his progressive clarification and legitimation of his Two-Kingdom idea of a worldly vocation in society as it is" ("German Mysticism in the Polarization of Ethical Behaviour," pp. 288, 289).

14. Karlstadt, "Whether One Should Proceed Slowly and Avoid Offending the Weak in Matters that Concern God's Will (1524)," reprinted in Sider, *Karlstadt's Battle with Luther*, p. 60.

15. *LW* 40, p. 207.

16. *LW* 31, p. 362.

17. For the role of the *imitatio* and *conformitas Christi* during the period of Karlstadt's so-called Wittenberg and Orlamünde theologies, see Ronald J. Sider, *Andreas Bodenstein von Karlstadt: The Development of His Thought 1517-1525*, Vol. XI of the series *Studies in Medieval and Reformation Thought*, ed. H. A. Oberman (Leiden: E. J. Brill, 1974), pp. 254-259.

18. Karlstadt, as quoted in Sider, *Andreas Bodenstein von Karlstadt*, p. 255.

19. *LW* 40, p. 85.

20. *Ibid.*

21. *Ibid.*, p. 149.

22. *Ibid.*

23. As reprinted in Sider, *Karlstadt's Battle with Luther*, p. 137.

24. On the issue of sin, for example, Karlstadt writes, "It is clear that sin is nothing other than willing otherwise than ... God wills" (Sider, *Karlstadt's Battle with Luther*, p. 213). The emphasis for Karlstadt is on obedience whereas for Luther, to act without faith is to sin. More will be said later concerning the role of the Holy Spirit.

25. James S. Preus writes, "The fundamental issues of 1521-1522 were issues of religious policy, and important aspects of the doctrinal profiles by which Lutheran and 'radical' are identified are as much a function of the religio-political struggle, and the result of reflection upon the outcome of that crisis, as they are a cause of the breakup of the movement .... To be sure, the theologies of Karlstadt and Luther were no means identical in 1521-1522, but neither were theological differences the decisive reason for their separation" (*Carlstadt's 'Ordinanciones' and Luther's Liberty: A Study of the Wittenberg Movement 1521-1522*, of the series *Harvard Theological Studies*, 27 (Cambridge, Mass.: Harvard University Press, 1974), p. 2).
    Ronald J. Sider agrees, arguing that the break between Luther and Karlstadt came "weil sie sich über Strategie, Taktik und Zeitplan von Reform nicht einig waren .... (In) 1522 stritten sie sich mehr über Strategie als über Theologie, und beides darf nicht miteinander verwechselt werden" ("Andreas Bodenstein von Karlstadt: Zwischen Liberalität und Radikalität," in *Radikale Reformatoren*, ed. Hans-Jürgen Goertz (München: C. H. Beck, 1978), p. 25).

26. Karlstadt, as quoted in Sider, *Andreas Bodenstein von Karlstadt*, p. 238.

27. *LW* 40, p. 87.

28. *LW* 31, p. 362.

29. Karlstadt, as quoted in Sider, *Karlstadt's Battle with Luther*, p. 128.

30. *Ibid.* The term "guzzlers" refers to Luther's renowned enjoyment of beer.

31. *Ibid.*, p. 55.

32. This is the famous public confrontation at the Black Bear Inn where Luther was staying. Karlstadt is recorded as saying to Luther, "Today in your

sermon Doctor, you attacked me somewhat severely and you interwove me in one number and work with the riotous murdering spirits, as you call them. I say 'No!' to that, although you charge the same spirits with a type of discourse about the living voice of God that I never heard from them in my day. But I do not say that because I want to defend them here. But I speak thus: He who wants to associate me and put me in the same pot with such murdering spirits ascribes that to me without truth and not as an honest man" ("What Dr. Andreas Bodenstein von Karlstadt Talked over with Dr. Martin Luther at Jena, and How They Have Decided to Write against Each Other," (1524), p. 40). For the entire transcript of the meeting, see Sider, *Karlstadt's Battle with Luther*, pp. 38-48. For an analysis of the debate and its historic background, see Rupp, *Patterns of Reformation*, pp. 131ff.

33. As quoted by Bainton, *Here I Stand*, p. 204.

34. *WA Br.* 785; translated and quoted by Bainton, *Here I Stand*, p. 205. See also *WA Br.* 797.

35. Disputes with the antinomian spiritualists and other groups with strong mystical tendencies were primarily, although not exclusively, concerned with issues such as pneumatology, revelation and human nature.

VIII. LUTHER AND THE ANABAPTISTS

A.   The Anabaptist Critique

- 1 -

Due to its theological pluralism and polygenesis, it is difficult to characterize the Anabaptist movement.[1] In one sense, the Anabaptists may be seen as the culmination and radicalization of the original evangelical vision of Luther, seeking to recreate without political or theological compromise the original New Testament church.[2] In another sense, they must also be considered as unique in that they maintained strains of scholasticism, Erasmian humanism and late medieval mystical theology, which, although originally accepted by Luther, he himself had come to disavow.[3]

The emphasis of the evangelical Anabaptists (Obenites, Dutch and Low German Mennonites) upon *gelassenheit*, the inward transformation of the self and experiential sanctification, was clearly within the tradition of Johannes Tauler and the restored *synteresis*. The Anabaptists from Balthasar Hübmaier (1480/85-1528) through Melchior Hoffmann (c. 1495-1543) maintained their understanding of the *synteresis* as a faculty, organ or inherent *substantia* in keeping with the medieval mystics and the pre-*fideist* Luther. Justification (*Rechtfertigung*) leading to experiential sanctification (*Gerechtmachung*) were conjoined by the Anabaptists as they were in traditional scholastic thought.

Luther and the Anabaptists

Sanctification has been made available to a fallen human nature by means of the sacrifice of Christ and the work of the Holy Spirit.[4] The passion of Christ is all-sufficient in and of itself in that it exculpated all humanity from sin;[5] however, Christ's death is efficacious as a basis for progressive sanctification only for those who maintain a repentant spirit and amend the external life by abandoning sin and making a positive effort to follow in Christ's steps by obeying the eternal will of God. The atoning sacrifice of Christ is for the 'unknown' sins of the individual (i.e., original and pre-baptismal sins before illumination). However the satisfaction made available by Christ's passion is operationally effective only through fulfilling the conditions of discipleship. These conditions included a practical asceticism and the obligation to bring forth good works according to the example of Christ. Although Christ has opened the gates to the Kingdom, by means of his suffering and death, his work is not complete.

The Anabaptists combined the mystics' impulse to die to self with the radicals' urge to imitate Christ unto the cross.[6] The conception of Christian discipleship, within the context of an inwardly experienced and externally manifested sanctification, had its source in the example of the life, works and death of Christ as portrayed in the Gospels.[7] While Christ was without question Redeemer, he was also the pre-eminent example of a truly Christian life.[8] The imitation of Christ, whether by means of good works or bearing the cross, was a necessary requirement for progressive sanctification. While the rewards of glorification and eternal salvation remained as eschatological promises, it still remains that the degree to which the elect obey the Word of God and imitate Christ is the measure to which they will overcome the powers of devil and hell in the perennial struggle against the forces of darkness.

While the imitation of Christ applied specifically to the piety of individual Christians, the Anabaptists also believed that the imitation of Christ carries with it the obligation to re-establish the true *ecclesia* along the lines of the primitive church as recorded in Scripture. The imitation of Christ as understood by the Anabaptists had radical ramifications for all society.[9] Within the framework of

132

'holiness' provided by a sanctified life and a sanctified community, Anabaptists could strive confidently for the progressive sanctification of individual and corporate life, with the *imitatio* providing specific guidelines along the way.

- 2 -

Given the centrality of a rigorously obedient discipleship to Anabaptist theology, some came to criticize Luther for the moral laxity they perceived among his followers. The radical reformation as a whole generally agreed that the palpable failure of the Lutheran reformation was its inability to change the moral life of its proponents. As one Anabaptist leader, a former Lutheran, as many among them were, was to say in 1538:

> I waited and hoped for a year or two since the minister had much to say of the amendment of life, of giving to the poor, loving one another and abstaining from evil. But I could not close my eyes to the fact that the doctrine which was preached and which was based on the Word of God, was not carried out. No beginning was made toward Christian living ....[10]

Although the Anabaptists looked to the congregations nearest to them rather than to what went on in Wittenberg, their charges were supported by Lutheran sources. Philip of Hesse claimed to see many more good works among Anabaptists than among Lutherans.[11] Luther considered the charges to be legitimate and accepted the criticism. In turn, he chastised his ministers. However Luther had also come to believe that the Anabaptists' criticism was a sure sign that they lacked the Holy Spirit which is patient with those who are 'weak in faith.'[12]

Luther understood the dilemma he and his ministers faced in the following way: "If works alone are taught -- as happened under the papacy, faith is lost. If faith alone is taught, unspiritual men will immediately suppose that works are not necessary."[13]

Luther and the Anabaptists

For the Anabaptists, the question of faith and works was not seen in the sharp antithetical terms in which Luther deemed to cast them in his continuing criticism of works-righteousness and defence of *sola fide, sola gratia*. When Melchior Rink, the leader of the Thüringian Anabaptists, criticized Lutherans for not performing good works, he argued that their absence was attributable to the absence of a doctrine of good works in Lutheran theology.[14] The South German Anabaptist leader, Hans Denck (c. 1495-1527), asks, "If works are ... to be rejected, why then does Paul say so earnestly (I Cor. 6:9f): No fornicator, no adulterer, no miser, no drunkard, no idolater will inherit the Kingdom of God?"[15] Luther was accused of bypassing the rigorous demands of the imitation of Christ and the voluntary bearing of the cross in order to preach the 'sweet Christ' and a faith which did not require that good works be done.[16] Luther turned to defend his stance on good works, arguing, "We do not ... reject good works; on the contrary, we cherish and teach them as much as possible."[17]

For scholasticism, salvation was the end product of morality. For the Anabaptists as well, the moral life and its works were intertwined with a belief in progressive sanctification.[18] In both cases, the theological framework provided the believers with a significant impetus to perform works. Compared to this, Luther's belief that 'faith alone justifies' combined with his warnings against purposeful striving were not regarded as providing the adherents with the proper motivation.

Hans Denck, a former Lutheran, had come to believe that Luther's *sola fide*, in fact, jeopardized the moral life of the Christian community. Denck, as Luther, began with the presupposition of faith but believed that faith can never be 'inherited belief' inculcated by one's parent. This hereditary faith is a 'false faith.' What is required is an inward faith which is outwardly confirmed by the believer's baptism.

Denck also takes up the Christological theme, criticizing Luther's doctrine of satisfaction.

> You say: 'Has not the head made satisfaction and fulfilled all that
> can be accomplished on behalf of the members?' Answer: Indeed,

134

He has made satisfaction and has levelled the path which no man could otherwise find that one may walk therein and reach life (Jn. 14:6). Whoever does not walk it, does not reach life; for him the path is useless. He has fulfilled the Law, not to place us above it, but to give us an example to follow Him (Jn. 13:15).[19]

For the Anabaptists, as for Karlstadt, it was obvious that works do not necessarily "issue spontaneously from faith" as Luther claimed.[20] It was not enough to recommend that "good works ought to be done."[21] The Christian faith not only advocated, but demanded a moral change of behaviour as evidence of a total transformation. This transformation was to be much more comprehensive than what they regarded as the mere forensic or declaratory justification offered by Luther and the '*solafideists.*'

Over against Luther's forensic justification through faith in the redemptive work of Christ, for the Anabaptists, the historic Christ, in his life and crucifixion, provided specific and normative instructions for proclaiming the Gospel of repentance. These, they felt, Luther was ignoring.[22] Caspar Schwenckfeld (1490-1561) argued that Luther's *solafideism* is the mistaken attempt "to bring more people to heaven than God wants there."[23] The key to the Christian life was not 'by faith alone,' but *nachfolge Christi.*[24]

Good works and right conduct, in imitation of Christ, initiated by Christ and measured against the example of Christ as recorded in Scripture, provided specific guidelines for Christian discipleship. The *imitatio* provided strict and rigorous demands for the individual and the community. Good works held the status of a necessary requirement of the Christian life, and were of far greater significance than the ethical consequence of a faith stance, to be done "as much as possible," as Luther maintained.[25] Luther's *sola fides justificat* by itself seemed to the Anabaptists not to be enough, for it could be, and in fact was, used by many Lutherans to do nothing -- a form of 'cheap grace.'[26] Balthasar Hubmaier charges that Luther's followers "find a girdle of fig leaves to cover their crimes and say 'Faith alone saves us and not our works.' (They) tell how their works are of no avail before God and therefore they at once let them go."[27] Common to all participants of the radical reformation was their disappointment

135

with Luther's apparent antipathy toward works and the consequent failure of the moral aspects of the Lutheran reformation. If works are seen to be an option within the Christian ethos, then being a Christian is merely a private sentiment at best and life remains unregenerate and fruitless.

B. Luther's Response

- 1 -

It was one thing to be criticized for not living up to the demands of doctrine. But when Luther felt his *sola fide. sola gratia* doctrine was in itself being criticized for making, or at least permitting, Christians to be "smug, lazy and sleepy,"[28] he responded angrily.

> All they (Anabaptists) do is to scream that good works ought to be done and that the law ought to be observed. All right, we know that, but because they are distinct topics, we will not permit them to be confused. In due time we shall discuss the teaching that the law and good works ought to be done.[29]

Luther still believed, as he had always believed, that right teaching led to right conduct. However, he rejected Karlstadt's and the Anabaptists' insistence on the evaluation of doctrine by the presence or absence of good works, or on how closely the life of the Christian, who is in faith conformed to Christ, imitates the life of Christ as revealed in Scripture. For Luther, "First there must be a tree, then the fruit."[30] The 'goodness' of works was to be evaluated by right relationship to God and by the doctrine which motivated them. But it did not follow, as Karlstadt and the Anabaptists claimed, that right conduct was a sign of right doctrine -- and right doctrine mattered more to Luther than did right conduct.

Although impressed by Anabaptist piety, Luther came to see all the radical reformers through his own bitter experiences with Karlstadt. Luther did not doubt for a moment that this same piety would lead the Anabaptists astray in their understanding of doctrine and would ultimately lead to a self-righteous pride and a minimizing of the free gift of God's grace. Christians are converted from unbelief to faith and not merely from moral laxity to moral earnestness and piety. In his commentary on Galatians 3:10-15 (1535), Luther writes:

> (I)t is a laudable and happy thing to unite the example of Christ in His deeds, to love one's neighbours, to do good to those who deserve evil, to pray for one's enemies, and to bear with patience the ingratitude of those who requite good with evil. But none of this contributes to righteousness in the sight of God .... Imitation of the example of Christ does not make us righteous in the sight of God.[31]

Luther had worked hard to separate faith and grace from works-righteousness and meritoriousness and his fear, whether justified or not, was that the Anabaptists were again linking them. Whenever criticized for a lack of good works by Lutherans, or the absence of a clearly defined doctrine of works, whether by Karlstadt or the Anabaptists, Luther in defence almost automatically associates the call to perform works with justification by works and works-righteousness.[32]

Luther is certainly familiar with the Scriptural passages which require good works of Christians and even remarks that these passages are innumerable. However, he never failed to point out that where these passages occur, especially in James, one hears little of the passion and resurrection of Christ. Luther felt that James ascribes justification to works when advocating works in addition to faith and he could not reconcile that position with Paul and the rest of Scripture.[33] Luther would have preferred to see this "epistle of straw"[34] excluded from New Testament canon.

Luther never denied, and oftentimes acknowledged, the fact that faith obliges or 'behooves' Christians to perform works in imitation of Christ. However, Luther makes little effort to advocate that Christians perform good works for fear of having it understood as supporting justification by works. Again and again Luther writes: "We do not deny that the example of Christ should be imitated by the godly and that good works must be done, but the pious do not become righteous in the sight of God on this account."[35]

- 2 -

For the Anabaptists, the progress of the reformation unleashed by Luther required that the precise form of good works, of the imitation of Christ and the example of Christ be clearly defined along Biblical lines. Putting aside for a moment the questions of works-righteousness and justification by works (which Luther seemed incapable of doing), and given the fact that both Luther and the so-called left-wing of the reformation, to a greater or lesser degree, advocated performing works in imitation of Christ, the question that has remained unresolved throughout is to what degree the example of Christ should provide normative guidance and direction for the Christian life.

Luther never clearly addressed the question, except to affirm that works of love should be faithfully performed and that the Christian must be faithfully willing to bear the cross. Specific examples of behaviour he considered of an exemplary nature were rare indeed. Luther never attempted to provide precise criteria or establish any but the most general guidelines. The reasons for this lack of specificity are simple.

First of all, the content of ethics and the precise form of the moral life had rarely been an issue prior to Luther's entry into European religious and political life. Conflicts among the medieval *viae* were seldom concerned with the question of the 'goodness' of a work in a moral sense, but rather disputed the 'goodness' of works in a meta-ethical or theological sense. In other words, disputes concerned questions of the function, status, role and value of good works and their relationship to righteousness, soteriology or the mind and will of God.

138

These were the issues Luther debated with scholasticism and the Roman Church. Questions of the precise content of good works or the specific form of the *Christus exemplum* were rarely raised within the medieval context.

Secondly, Luther was always hesitant to speak of the third use of the law (*tertius usus legis*), for fear of placing the faithful once again under the constraints of the law. The law performs a twofold function. The first function is 'civil,' that is, the law preserves order, justice and peace in the world.[36] The second function of the law, the 'spiritual,' is more indirect. The law performs God's work in that it accuses and condemns the sinner and reveals unrighteousness in all. But obedience to the law does not make Christians righteous before God.[37] Normative guidelines for Christian conduct would have been regarded by Luther as too closely aligned with the *tertius usus legis*.

Finally, Luther's reticence in clearly delineating the *Christus exemplum* along scriptural lines may be attributable to the fact that he did not subscribe to a literalist *sola scriptura*.[38] It is illegitimate to conclude that because Christ was a man, therefore the clergy must be male, or, because Christ is assumed to have been celibate, that therefore the clergy must also be celibate.[39] Although there are some marked exceptions (which will be examined later), in most cases Luther did not believe "that incidental circumstances and external detail are to be strictly binding."[40] We have no way of knowing which characteristics or actions of the historical Jesus are contingent to the particular circumstances and which transcend their time and place and have relevance for us. In other words, Scripture does not in itself provide principles for determining which examples are to be regarded as normative and binding upon us and which are not.

The Anabaptist emphasis upon good works, their rigorously upheld standard of the imitation of Christ and attempt to delineate clearly the example of Christ along Biblical lines were considered by Luther to be a return to the strictures of the law. They represented a legalism grounded in Biblical literalism. To take this line of reasoning to a *reductio ad absurdum*, this would require the wearing of robes and sandals and living in Palestine.[41]

Luther and the Anabaptists

Scripture cannot provide standard norms which prescribe specific actions, for then it would cease to be the Gospel and become a new law. Scripture does not provide a rationale for ideology or the structure of social organization. Responding to the use of Biblical examples, Luther writes, "We will admit no example, not even from Christ Himself, for it must be accompanied by God's Word which explains to us in what sense we are to follow or not to follow it."[42]

In his doctrine of the Word, Luther distinguished sharply between law and Gospel, the former being essentially command, the latter being promise. The law is necessary to remind Christians of the need for grace as promised in the Gospels. However the grace of God demands the response of faith. It is the faithful acceptance of God's graceful presence which lies at the heart of the Christian experience rather than the slavish emulation of externals and particulars.

Christians are called to the spontaneous activity allowed by a freed conscience. By virtue of one's faith in the promise of the *verbum Dei*, the self is set free to act. The moral legitimacy of actions must not be determined by the strictures of the law but solely in order to avoid the wrath of God and fulfill the needs of the neighbour. Christians are not bound to the tyrannical rigours of the law as expressed in the heteronomous words of Scripture, but if in faith conformed to Christ by the activity of the Spirit, live in theonomous creativity.

To codify Christ is to trap him in history with little relevance to contemporary life except as a moral authority from out of the past, deserving respect, but not adoration and worship. To codify and prescribe the imitation of Christ in terms of particulars and rigid norms is to turn Christology into ideology, at which point the Spirit is silenced and faith is dead. For, without the reality of the Spirit, the Word is only law; without faith, works have no meaning; and without the *Christus sacramentum*, Christ is merely a prophet. So it is with the imitation of Christ. Without the reality of the Spirit, the *imitatio* becomes merely a law and a prescription for living rather than the joyful experience of inner freedom in God's presence.

- 3 -

While it is generally considered as central to his dispute with the antinomian spiritualists rather than the Anabaptists, it may be of value to examine briefly Luther's understanding of the guidance offered by the Holy Spirit and freedom of conscience, particularly as these relate to good works and the imitation of Christ.

In order to understand Luther's concept of the conscience, it is necessary to return to the previous discussion of the *synteresis*.[43] For Gabriel Biel, the *synteresis* was the 'spark' which provided the ontological foundation for the conscience. The conscience in turn directed or 'inclined' the will to perform good works. For the young Luther, the *synteresis* was also located within the conscience, but rather than providing the will with a natural inclination toward good, just and right activity, Luther argued that the *synteresis* was the "witnessing portion" (*superstite portione*)[44] of the conscience. That is, the *synteresis* is the source of the complaint the conscience makes when the will has chosen something other than that which it should.[45] The conscience condemns the action *post facto* and with it the agent who initiated the action.[46]

Luther's developing notion of human nature as entirely corrupted by sin entailed his rejection of the *synteresis*. The belief that one's actions are the direct outward manifestation of an inner righteousness effectively stills the activity of the conscience. While rejecting the *synteresis* in favour of a Spirit-engendered faith, Luther nevertheless did retain his concept of the conscience. However, in that the conscience is a prisoner of sin as well, it cannot in and of itself witness to good, just and right activity. It is the Spirit-mediated presence of Christ which witnesses to good, just and right activity, thereby enabling the conscience to judge ourselves and our actions and to condemn the self when we place our own self-interest before the needs of another.

Luther and the Anabaptists

Good works are only possible as a result of the presence of the Holy Spirit. However, it must be pointed out that this is not the same as claiming that the Holy Spirit directs our actions. For Luther, the Holy Spirit must not be understood as a supernatural or transcendent causality which endows the self with a new nature, faculty or attribute. The Spirit does not infuse love, thereby imbuing the self with a new habit of mind (*infusio caritatis*),[47] as in the *synteresis* tradition of late medieval mysticism and scholasticism.

The will remains in bondage to sin.[48] However, in granting justification and promising forgiveness, the Holy Spirit sets the conscience free to accuse and condemn self-will. In mediating the presence of Christ, the Spirit offers the faithful hope in the midst of despair, joy in the midst of suffering, courage in the midst of fear, strength in the midst of infirmity and freedom in the midst of bondage. All these gifts we receive through faith, and all are necessary to enable the conscience to witness to good, just and right activity.

In setting the conscience free, the Spirit permits a moral life. But it does not automatically provide instruction, teaching or perception, nor does it direct the self to perform particular works. Luther rejected the unmediated autodidacticism of a Divine-inspiration pneumatology as advocated by the Enthusiasts.[49] The Spirit sets the conscience free to make moral choices which may not be in the immediate best interests of the self; but the Spirit does not make our choices for us. To claim the direct guidance or teaching of the Holy Spirit is to be absolved of responsibility for our actions (as incidentally is the consequence of a narrow legalism as well). However, to reject responsibility is to deny the continuing corruption of self-will and complicity in evil. This recognition of one's corruption and complicity is only possible because in witnessing to good, just and right activity the Spirit has given the conscience the ability to accuse and condemn the self. Without the presence of the Spirit, the conscience is stilled, there is no basis for guilt and remorse, no need to take refuge in Christ and no internal struggle which signifies that one is "at one and the same time a sinner and righteous."[50]

142

It is because the Spirit frees the conscience that any theology which emphasizes pneumatology may be prone to exhibit tendencies toward antinomianism, as Luther saw displayed in the spiritualists. It is precisely for this reason that the imitation of Christ again becomes significant. While the Holy Spirit provides the freedom, hope, strength, courage and joy to perform works and bear the cross, it is not the Spirit but the example of Christ which offers guidance and provides Christians with normative criteria for moral action. The law faithfully observed prevents the abuse of freedom. For example, over against what he considered were wrong beliefs concerning baptism, the sacraments and other aspects of liturgy, Luther held that "we must resolutely set the words and examples of Christ."[51]

Despite concessions to a Spirit-engendered freedom of conscience, Luther believed that the example of Christ can provide specific guidance for Christian conduct. In his *Misuse of the Mass* (1521), Luther takes a stance entirely compatible with the use of Biblical examples in Anabaptist theology when he writes: "Now the more closely our Mass resembles that first Mass of all, which Christ performed at the Last Supper, the more Christian it will be."[52] And further:

> (I)t would not be advisable for a Christian person to deviate from the example of Christ and make innovations in such important matters without an example. Why did Christ show us the way with His words and works, and preach to us, if we are permitted to undertake or begin anything without His words and work? Why did He come into the world at all if it is not sufficient for us to follow Him in that which He taught us? .... This (to make a sacrifice of the sacrament) is not merely to act without example; it is contrary to the word and example of Christ -- something which even Christian freedom cannot excuse, since it is the most damnable idolatry and blasphemy.[53]

In his disputations with the Anabaptists, Luther recognized the dangers of an indiscriminate exemplarism and the need for important distinctions. While Christians, particualry in matters of doctrine, are never to act contrary to the example of Christ -- 'which even Christian freedom cannot excuse' -- Christians are not obliged to imitate all the works of Christ. The words and examples of Christ provide a standard against which an informed conscience can stand in judgment, as we are judged by God. While the Anabaptists tended to reject whatever the Bible did not enjoin,[54] Luther would allow whatever Scripture did not prohibit. Luther's doctrine of the imitation of Christ was intended to provide the guidance and direction of a compass, while maintaining a *libertas in externis*; the Anabaptists were providing a map.

Luther's exemplarism was directed primarily, although not exclusively, to supporting a religious attitude rather than providing concrete examples of the Christian life and its good works.[55] Again, Luther emphasizes that it is not an external act which is to be repeated, but an internal attitude which is to be manifested. Christians are called to imitate the paradigmatic pattern of Christ's life. Christians are to have faith in the midst of bearing the cross and to serve the needs of the neighbour faithfully, not as it is displayed in Jesus, but because it is displayed in Jesus. Be obedient, humble and loving, not *as* he was, for we all live in different situations and contexts, but *because* he was.

Luther thus reaffirms what he established early in his career with his *imitatio mentis, imitatio operis* distinction, namely, that certain features of the example of Christ are of no significance to the Christian in that they are in fact particular traits of the historical Jesus. Rather than specific words or examples derived from the life of Christ, it is the intentionality and motivation which animated Christ which must be stressed.

While it is, of course, not axiomatic that a more clearly defined, Biblically-informed vision of Christian discipleship will necessarily lead to a self-righteous pride and a minimizing of the free gift of God's grace, as Luther feared, nevertheless, it still remains that the detailed attempt to live as Jesus did does not constitute a 'proper' imitation in accordance with Luther's criteria. Luther held that only the *imitatio mentis*, with its 'concern for the spirit,' can prevent the imitation of Christ from becoming a ritualistic, ascetic or ideological prescription.

NOTES

1. The term Anabaptist or *Wiedertäufer* was a pejorative term used by German and Swiss state-church reformers to characterize various sectarian Protestant groups, including the Swiss, Mennonite and Hutterian Brethren among others. This characterization was significant in that it placed these 'rebaptisers' under the strictures of an ancient Roman law against rebaptism (Code of Justinian), and made them liable to official state persecution and ultimately the death penalty (originally used against the Donatists). Many of the various radical groups that the label was applied to never accepted the term themselves and many thus designated do not fit into this category. See Franklin H. Littel, *The Origins of Sectarian Protestantism* (Toronto: Collier-Macmillan, 1964), pp. IX-XVI.

Luther, as well, can be criticized for misrepresenting the Anabaptists. He sometimes confused them with the Schwärmer, the antinomian spiritualists and Libertines, accusing them of too pronounced an emphasis upon pneumatology resulting in an excessive subjectivism and spiritualism. At other times, and perhaps closer to the mark, he considered their emphasis upon clearly delineating the example of Christ along Biblical lines as a return to literalism and legalism resulting in a denial of the Spirit. See John S. Oyer, "The Writings of Luther Against the Anabaptists," *Mennonite Quarterly Review*, 27 (1953), pp. 100-110.

The intent of this section is not to examine the entire range of Anabaptist theology nor to justify or question the validity of Luther's dispute with 'the radicals.' Whether Luther is correct in his assessment of his opponents or whether he misrepresented them is of interest and deserving of examination, but will not be dealt with in this work. Rather, the focus will be limited to determining how Luther's perception of the Anabaptists, whether accurate or not, shaped his own understanding of faith, good works and the imitation of the example of Christ, with the sole objective being to illuminate more clearly Luther's thought concerning these issues.

2. See H. S. Bender, "The Anabaptist Vision," *Church History*, 13 (1944), pp. 3-24, reprinted in *The Anabaptists and Thomas Müntzer*, ed. J. M. Stayer (Dubuque/Toronto: Kendall/Hunt Publishing Co., 1980), pp. 13-22.

3. See Jarold K. Zeman, "Anabaptism: A Replay of Medieval Themes or a Prelude to the Modern Age?," *Mennonite Quarterly Review*, 50 (1976), pp. 266ff.; and H. Fast, "The Dependence of the First Anabaptists on Luther, Erasmus and Zwingli," *Mennonite Quarterly Review*, 30 (1956), pp. 104-119.

4. Some, including Balthasar Hubmaier, held that the *gemüt* or *apex mentis* was not even directly involved in the Fall. See Williams, "German Mysticism in the Polarization of Ethical Behaviour," pp. 292-295.

5. This aspect of Anabaptist universality is especially pronounced in Melchior Hoffmann. See Williams, "German Mysticism in the Polarization of Ethical Behaviour," pp. 285, 300-301.

6. See Keneth R. Davis, *Anabaptism and Asceticism: A Study in Intellectual Origins* (Scottsdale, Penn.: Herald Press, 1974), pp. 24ff.

7. See Zeman, "Anabaptism," pp. 266ff.

8. See Oyer, "The Writings of Luther Against the Anabaptists," pp. 215ff.

9. For the Anabaptists, as with Thomas Müntzer, the imitation of Christ and revolutionary social transformation are complementary rather than antithetical concepts. Referring specifically to Müntzer, Carl E. Braaten argues that the effect of the imitation of Christ was akin to "planting dynamite charges in the social structure" ("Theologie der Revolution!," *Lutherische Monatshefte*, 5 (1968), p. 215). Hans-Jürgen Goertz, referring to Müntzer as well, observes that the *imitatio* "has as its goal the transformation of the 'world' or its annihilation .... Discipleship is a mystical-revolutionary act" ("The Mystic With the Hammer: Thomas Müntzer's Theological Basis for Revolution," *Mennonite Quarterly Review*, 50 (1976), p. 103).
    Although Müntzer cannot be unqualifiedly grouped with the Anabaptists, who did not share the aspirations toward theocracy characteristic of the revolutionary spiritualism of the Zwickau prophets, nevertheless, in his renunciation of Luther's *sola fide* and emphasis on suffering, the cross and 'the bitter Christ,' he is closely aligned to the evangelical Anabaptists whom he doubtlessly influenced in this regard. See J. M. Stayer and W. O. Packull, ed., *The Anabaptists and Thomas Müntzer, passim*.
    The universal evangelical social implications of Anabaptist theology were held in check after witnessing the defeat of the peasants' revolt and experiencing their own persecution. Rather than change the world, the true *ecclesia* now had to separate itself from the affairs of the world.

10. Anonymous, as quoted in Bender, "The Anabaptist Vision," p. 15.

11. See Bainton, *Here I Stand*, p. 295.

12. See Harry Loewen, *Luther and the Radicals: Another Look at Some Aspects of the Struggle Between Luther and the Radical Reformers* (Waterloo: Wilfrid Laurier University Press, 1974), pp. 91ff.

13. *LW* 27, p. 63; *WA* 40 II, p. 78; see also *LW* 27, p. 48; *WA* 40 II, p. 60.

14. See John S. Oyer, *Lutheran Reformers Against Anabaptists: Luther, Melanchthon and Menius and the Anabaptists of Central Germany* (The Hague: Martinus Nijhoff, 1964), pp. 77-78.

15. Hans Denck, *Whether God is the Cause of Evil*, (1526) as reprinted in *Spiritual and Anabaptist Writers: Documents Illustrative of the Radical Reformation*, ed. George H. Williams, Vol. XXV of *The Library of Christian Classics* (Philadelphia: Westminster Press, 1957), p. 105.

16. The term originates with Müntzer who argued that the 'sweet' Christ of faith can be known only if the believer has also experienced the 'bitter' Christ of suffering. According to Müntzer, what must be preached is "the whole of and not merely the half of Christ. He who does not wish to accept the bitter Christ will eat himself sick of honey" ("Von dem gedichteten Glauben," (1523) as quoted by George H. Williams, *The Radical Reformation* (Philadelphia: Westminster Press, 1962), p. 51). The Anabaptists adopted Müntzer's criticism of Lutherans. See Oyer, *Lutheran Reformers Against Anabaptists*, pp. 19, 222-223.

17. *LW* 31, p. 363.

18. Luther saw the tension between *temporalia* and *aeterna* or *externa* and *interna* or *peccator* and *iustus* in terms of paradox. The Anabaptists saw these opposites in terms of moral progress. The responsibility of the Christian was to move from one to the other.

19. Hans Denck, *The Law of God*, (1526) as reprinted in *Selected Writings of Hans Denck*, ed. and trans. E. J. Furcha and F. L. Battles, in *Pittsburgh Original Texts and Translation Series*, 1 (Pittsburgh: Pickwick Press, 1975), p. 49.

20. *WA* 57 III, p. 114; see also *LW* 27, p. 96; *WA* 40 II, p. 121.

21. *LW* 26, p. 145.

22. George H. Williams writes, "They (Anabaptists) understood the imitation of Christ, from hazardous rebaptism at some Germanic Jordan to a martyr's pyre, (as) representing the fulness of the Christian way" ("Introduction," *The Library of Christian Classics*, XXV, p. 30).

23. Caspar Schwenckfeld, *Corpus Schwenkfeldianorium*, IV, p. 834 as quoted by Williams, *Radical Reformation*, p. 107.

24. See Bender, "The Anabaptist Vision," p. 17.

25. *LW* 31, p. 363.

26. The charge of 'cheap grace' was originally made by Müntzer and taken up by other members of the radical reformation. See Steven Ozment's analysis of Müntzer's critique of Luther in *Mysticism and Dissent*, pp. 66ff.

27. Balthasar Hubmaier, *On Free Will* (1527), as reprinted in *The Library of Christian Classics*, XXV, p. 115.

28. *LW* 26, p. 143.

29. *Ibid.*, p. 145 (1535).

30. *Ibid.*, p. 255; *WA* 40 I, p. 402. Luther avoids the complementary verse in Matthew 7:19, "Every tree that does not bear good fruit is cut down and thrown into the fire" (RSV).

31. *LW* 26, p. 247.

32. Joseph Lortz attributes Luther's 'knee-jerk reaction' to works-righteousness to "the very real trauma of works-righteousness which followed Luther out of the cloister" ("The Basic Elements of Luther's Intellectual Style," p. 27).

33. *LW* 35, pp. 395ff.

34. *WA DB* 6, p. 10.

35. *LW* 26, p. 146.

36. "We ought to proclaim the law and its works, not for Christians, but for the crude and unbelieving. For among Christians we must use the law spiritually (i.e., to reveal sin). But among the crude masses, on Mr. Everyman, we must use it boldly and roughly, so that they know what works of the law they are to do and what works ought to be left undone. Thus they are compelled by sword and law to be outwardly pious, much in the manner in which we control wild animals with chains and pens, so that external peace will exist among the people. To this end temporal authority is ordained, which God would have us honour and fear. (Rom. 13 [:1]; 1 Pet. 3) [1 Peter 2:13, 17]" *LW* 40, p. 83.

37. See *LW* 26, p. 39; *WA* 40 I, p. 479.

38. Both the *sola scriptura* and the *tertius usus legis* were developed by the second generation of the Lutheran reformation. See Oberman, "Headwaters of the Reformation," pp. 48ff.

39. The example of Christ is still used as a basis for these beliefs in some branches of the Christian faith. See Pius XII, *Sacra Virginitas*, 17 (1954); John XXIII, *Sacerdotii Nostri Primordia*, 16 (1959); Paul VI, *Sacerdotalis Coelibatus*, 26 (1967).

40. *LW* 40, pp. 132-133.

41. See Jeremy Moiser, "Dogmatic Thoughts on the Imitation of Christ," *Scottish Journal of Theology*, 30, pp. 201-213.

42. *LW* 40, p. 132.

43. See pp. 18-21 of this work.

44. *WA* 1, p. 36.

45. See Baylor, *Action and Person*, p. 168. See also Bernard Lohse, "Conscience and Authority in Luther," in *Luther and the Dawn of the Modern Era: Papers for the Fourth International Congress for Luther Research* (Leiden: E. J. Brill, 1974), pp. 158-183.

46. Luther was also aware of the antecedent function of the conscience which warns the agent of an act that should not be performed. However, Luther was more concerned with the consequential function of the conscience which he himself had experienced. As the source of guilt pangs and feelings of remorse, the conscience serves a theological function in allowing the self to recognize its own sinfulness which in turn forces the self to turn in faith to Christ in its distress-filled plea for forgiveness. Cf. Krister Stendahl, "The Apostle Paul and the Introspective Conscience of the West," *Harvard Theological Review*, 55 (1963), pp. 119-215.

47. Prenter, *Spiritus Creator*, pp. 19, 26-27.

48. See especially Luther's *Bondage of the Will* (1526), *WA* 18, pp. 600-787; *LW* 33, pp. 3-295.

49. *LW* 27, p. 20; *WA* 40 II, p. 23. See also Robert Bertram, "The Radical Dialectic Between Faith and Works in Luther's Lectures on Galatians (1535)," in *Luther for an Ecumenical Age: Essays in Commemoration of the 450th Anniversary of the Reformation*, ed. Carl S. Meyer (St. Louis: Concordia, 1967), esp. pp. 228ff.

50. *WA* 56, p. 70.

51. *LW* 36, p. 51.

52. *Ibid.*, p. 52.

53. *Ibid.*, pp. 52-53.   Although his use of Biblical examples is entirely compatible with their use in Anabaptist theology, the Anabaptists were not particularly pleased with Luther's usage in this specific case.   Luther was criticized by the revolutionary or charismatic spiritualists, notably Sebastian Franck, as a literalist "who wish(es) to understand Scripture according to the Letter." See Sebastian Franck, *A Letter to John Campanus*, (1531), reprinted in *The Library of Christian Classics*, XXV, p. 157.

54. Conrad Grebel writes that "whatever we are not taught by clear passages or examples must be regarded as forbidden, just as if it were written."   See Conrad Grebel, *Letter to Thomas Müntzer*, (1524), reprinted in *The Library of Christian Classics*, XXV, p. 75.

55. John M. Headley argues that, "An analysis of Luther's distinctions in types of examples and his qualified use of the concomitant idea of imitation indicates that his exemplarism was directed more to supporting a religious attitude than to providing moral norms for individual cultivation" (*Luther's View of Church History*, p. 47).

IX. *FIDES ABSTRACTA, FIDES INCARNATA*

Following his break with scholasticism and throughout the course of his career, Luther consistently denied the soteriological efficacy of good works and the imitation of the *Christus exemplum*. Good works must issue spontaneously from faith without the self-serving presumption of righteousness or need for merit and reward. Only faith can make our works good. Faith alone justifies our being and our actions. Faith is the necessary requirement and precondition of good works.

Luther often stated that 'good works follow faith,' and, on the basis of Matt. 7:18, that "the good tree bears the good fruits."[1] This particular understanding of faith and works, originally formulated in the context of Luther's dispute with the Roman Church, was highly effectual in countering what Luther considered were exaggerated claims made on behalf of works by scholasticism. It was a position that Luther held consistently throughout his career. However, in suggesting this sequential ordering of faith and works, we are left with a semantic difficulty, to say the least. The phrase, 'works follow faith,' is not prescriptive but is essentially descriptive in character. In and of itself, it provides little guidance for the adherents of Luther's theology.

When it came to disputes with his own followers and other reformers, Luther was forced to a reexamination of his doctrine of faith and works. This resulted, not in a reevaluation of his doctrine, but in an elaboration, or more accurately, several elaborations. It is precisely at this point of elaboration that several significant ambiguities and inconsistencies in Luther's understanding of faith and works are revealed.

- 2 -

At times, Luther maintains that "faith is followed by works as the body is followed by its shadow."[2] This following is so integral that it becomes "impossible to separate works from faith, quite as impossible as to separate heat and light from fire."[3] There is within trees an inner need to bear fruit, and an inner necessity within fire to produce heat and light. It is a part of their natural existence. It is what they were meant to do. Act and being are inextricably intertwined.

Similarly, within the Christian faith exists an engendering inner spontaneity which transmutes the extrinsically imposed 'thou shalt' of the law, to an inner longing -- an 'I must.'[4] Luther argues that faith and works cannot be separated. For faith to be real it has to be put into practise. For faith to be real it has to be active. Christians must faithfully perform works. Faith must lead to good works. Works are the external manifestation of an inward faith. Luther writes:

> We should not simply think 'All I have to do is to believe and everthing is taken care of, I do not have to do any good works.' No, we must not separate the two. You must do good works and help your neighbour so that faith may shine outwardly in life as it shines inwardly in the heart.[5]

When advised that his own followers were not performing works, Luther took a stronger stand, arguing that this following of works from faith is so integral to the very meaning of faith that works provide the external validation of an inward faith. In fact, "Whoever does not do such good works is an unbeliever," writes Luther. "He gropes and looks around for faith and good works but knows neither what faith is or what good works are."[6] Works are the outward manifestation, concretion and validation of a genuine faith. The fruits 'bear testimony' to the

152

tree which produces them.[7] "(I)f good works do not follow it is certain that this faith in Christ does not dwell in our heart."[8]

At times, Luther's understanding of the relationship between faith and works achieves a synthesis of mutual complementarity. Faith is necessary for works, but without works there can be no true faith. Works of love are a necessary component of the very meaning of faith. Love of the neighbour is understood as the inherent natural consequence of the structure of faith itself.[9] The *necessitas* aspect, the theological impetus to act, is preserved within Luther's conception of *sola fide* as a *fides incarnata*. Faith is thereby denied the status of a universal Protestant virtue in its own right and it becomes illegitimate to conceive of faith as, itself, a good work.[10] This understanding of *sola fide* as *fides incarnata* clearly invalidates the critique of Luther's doctrine of faith and works made by Karlstadt and the Anabaptists.

- 3 -

Luther did not, however, retain his understanding of *sola fide* as a *fides incarnata* throughout the course of his career. At times Luther places such an emphasis upon faith, the *Christus sacramentum* and *conformitas Christi*, that good works, the *Christus exemplum* and the *imitatio Christi*, become severely depreciated in his thought.

Luther had persistent reservations regarding the conjoining or intertwining of faith and works and this concern remained paramount.[11] As was pointed out in the exposition of his concept of *Beruf*, Luther held that Christ does not concern himself with politics or economics.[12] This was a stance Luther held consistently. Ironically, particularly during the period of his disputes with Karlstadt and the Anabaptists, where one would expect reconciliatory statements, Luther specifically isolated the Christian faith from *praxis* with his pronouncement that "The Gospel does not become involved in the affairs of the world ...."[13] Faith requires an unconditional trust in the unaided power of the Word.

Whoever does not perform good works need not despair. It is still possible for faith to be genuine even if works of love do not flow from it, for the central message of the Gospel remains that we should hold to Christ solely by means of our faith. Genuine faith, by which we receive justification and salvation, is all that is required of Christians and genuine faith continues to be defined as pure receptivity to the promise of God and pure passivity to the will of God. The genuine faith by which we are granted Christ's 'alien' righteousness is nothing other than a confession of absolute dependency. Christian righteousness "is passive and we receive it."[14] All that is required of Christians is to "cling in faith to this one man, Christ -- that is the sufficient and necessary condition."[15]

While at times Luther allows for the possibility of a faith without works, at other times he is much more emphatic in asserting an antithetical relationship between faith and works. "Faith does not perform works, it believes in Christ."[16] Works of love must be 'put aside'; "all that is kept is faith, which justifies and makes alive."[17] It is from this perspective that Luther rebukes the Anabaptists for even suggesting that Christians "must suffer many things ... and imitate the example of Christ,"[18] preferring instead to argue that faith "learns about Christ and grasps Him without having to bear the cross."[19]

As a result of his elaboration of *sola fide* as a *fides abstracta* Luther was severely criticized by Karlstadt and the Anabaptists for advocating forensic justification, 'cheap' grace, a 'sweet' Christ and a privation or spiritualization of faith. Such a person reduces works to an option within the Christian ethos which ultimately transforms faith into a form of quietism.

Sola fide, if understood in the sense of a *fides abstracta*, threatens to tear works from its correlate of faith. A strong emphasis on faith alone, without a similar stress on the need to express that faith through good works, removes the element of *necessitas*, relegating works to the status of an option within the

Christian ethos. The *fides abstracta* makes of the God-relationship entirely an internal, personal matter, which means that the realm of morality remains largely unaffected by faith.[20] One's relationship to God comes to be seen as having priority over one's relationship to the neighbour, to the point of its exclusion. The willingness to perform works and bear the cross has become separated from faith. This, however, is to spiritualize faith and bifurcate the Christian life, divorcing the Gospel from the affairs of the world. If *sola fide* is understood in the sense of a *fides abstracta*, then the critiques by Karlstadt and the Anabaptists, in regard to Luther's 'sweet Christ,' 'phoney faith,' 'cheap grace' and 'forensic justification,' must be taken seriously and regarded as valid.

- 4 -

Luther's single-minded determination combined with the prophetic simplicity of his central themes of faith and grace (not to minimize their profundity) lose some of their impact when they are examined closely and tested in the concrete realm of human affairs. Luther's negative thesis, namely, that there is no justification by works, remains constant throughout his career, as does his belief that faith precedes works. But, his attempt to provide a positive theological foundation for Christian discipleship is fraught with inconsistencies, ambiguities and confusion. Luther never tired of saying, especially in his disputations with the antinomian spiritualists, that "faith without works is dead,"[21] while at the same time ridiculing the Anabaptists for their belief that "faith without works is dead."[22]

At one point, Luther appears to have become quite confused as to where he stood. Take, for example, the desperate attempt to integrate faith and works, evident in the following reference.

> (W)e, too say that faith without works is worthless and useless. The papists and fanatics take this to mean faith without works does not justify, or that if faith does not have works, it is of no

155

> avail, no matter how true it is. That is false. But faith without works -- that is a fantastic idea and mere vanity and a dream of the heart -- it is a false faith and does not justify.[23]

In the same statement Luther claims that the 'papists and fanatics' belief that "faith without works does not justify" is false, yet by the end of the paragraph he is himself arguing that "faith without works ... is a false faith and does not justify." In the same statement Luther rejects the *fides incarnata* when advocated by the papists and fanatics yet affirms his own *fides incarnata*.

- 5 -

The same intensity of debate and inconsistency and confusion evident in his understanding of the relationship between faith and works, which characterized Luther's career, was to become one of the characteristics of the movement which succeeded him. After Luther's death in 1546, the second generation of the Lutheran reformation experienced decades of internecine conflict which threatened to destroy the legacy Luther left.[24]

One of the distinctive features of the second generation of the Lutheran reformation was the polarization which occurred around the issue of faith and works. The Gnessio-Lutherans, who claimed to be the true followers of Luther, became radicalized to the point where they could argue that not only are good works not required of Christians, but they may, in fact, even be harmful for one's salvation (Nickolaus von Amsdorf). Another faction went so far as to claim that good works are necessary for salvation (Georg Major). The claims of both extremes were, of course, illegitimate when compared to any of Luther's statements, as was to be recognized during the series of negotiations culminating in the Formula of Concord (1577).[25] While the claims of both extremes may have been illegitimate, both factions, nevertheless, must be regarded as legitimate heirs of Luther's apparent inability to come to terms with the issue of faith and works.[26]

156

Why this ambiguity and inconsistency in the very heart of Luther's thought?   One possible approach is to deny that any real conflict exists.   An argument can be made that Luther changed throughout his life, moving from one understanding to the next in a developmental or chronological sequence, with statements made in support of one side belonging to an early so-called 'Catholic' Luther, while those supporting the other side belong to the 'mature' Luther.[27] The historical facts do not support this view.

During his disputations with Karlstadt and the Anabaptists, Luther rejected the radical reformation's emphasis on performing works in imitation of the example of Christ, preferring instead to place his stress upon *sola fide, sola gratia* and the *Christus sacramentum*. His statement that "faith does not perform works, it believes in Christ,"[28] is clearly within his understanding of *sola fide* as *fides abstracta*. However, in the continuing attacks by the Roman Church (which were at their height just prior to and during his dispute with Karlstadt), and in his critique of the antinomian spiritualists (which occurred during and just after his disputations with the Anabaptists), Luther maintained the same complementary *sacramentum et exemplum, conformitas* and *imitatio* and faith and 'good works' positions characteristic of his *fides incarnata*.

The stages of Luther's thought do not follow one another in a progressive, chronological development.   Luther's emphasis upon either a *fides incarnata* or a *fides abstracta* during different stages of his career cannot be dismissed by an analysis of his writings which claims a distinction between a 'young' and 'mature' Luther.   There is no evidence of a consistent, progressive development of Luther's doctrine of faith and works.

Given this lack of evidence within Luther's writings for a consistent, progressive development (at least in regard to his understanding of the relationship between faith and works), another explanation for Luther's inconsistency may be entertained. The argument is that in his attempt to give his thesis the greatest possible force and impact, particularly in the heat of disputes, Luther was prone to overstatements, unrestrained exaggeration and superlativism. It may be argued that those statements Luther made in support of a *fides abstracta* are extreme representations of just such a type. These statements were in fact overreactions and do not represent the true or essential Luther.

This hypothesis leaves the historian with a serious problem. More is at stake here than mere accentuation. This hypothesis offers no basis for determining which is the primary position and which is an aberration. Rhetorical flourishes and linguistic excesses may be excused except when the integrity of the content is in itself threatened by those excesses. The discrepancies in Luther's thought represent more than the excesses of polemical tone and rhetoric but point to an inconsistency within his understanding of the content of the life of faith itself.

Ultimately, the distinction between an 'essential' Luther and an 'overreactionary' Luther is no more tenable or satisfying as a means by which to determine which doctrine of faith and works Luther actually advocated than was the distinction between the 'young' and 'mature' Luther. Both forms of faith are compatible with Luther's one consistent position, namely, that faith precedes works. Attempts at further elaboration reveal discrepancies within Luther's statements that must be acknowledged as pointing to an inconsistency in his thought. The ambiguities one observes reach into the heart of Luther's theology -- into the centre of what he understands by faith.

- 7 -

In order to understand the inconsistencies within Luther's doctrine of faith and works, it may be of value to reexamine the sources of Luther's doctrine in an attempt to determine whether the discrepancies referred to were created during

158

the period of his disputes with the second generation of the reformation, or whether these discrepancies were inherent within Luther's doctrine from the time of its original inception, and only became readily apparent as a result of his elaboration.

One of the sources of Luther's doctrine of works lies in his original acceptance of the *obedientia activa* as advocated by Gabriel Biel and the nominalist tradition. The task of the Christian was to persevere in righteousness and to obey and actualize the will of God through good works performed in imitation of the *Christus exemplum.* Luther's discovery of Augustine's anti-Pelagian thesis and his development of *sola gratia* led to his criticism and ultimate rejection of the righteousness and meritoriousness of works. However, while denying the soteriological efficacy of works, Luther never disputed the fact that the faithful are to actively perform good works in imitation of the example of Christ.

The second primary source of Luther's doctrine of faith and works lay in the tradition of Germanic mystical theology. This tradition stressed the faithful, suffering, humiliated example of Christ as the paradigmatic form of the Christian life. The imitation of Christ was characterized as entailing an *obedientia passiva.* The Christian's task was to suffer and bear the cross, be passive, be resigned to the will of God and place one's absolute trust in God's omnipotence and omniscience, as did Christ.

Luther's deepening understanding of the nature of sin together with his developing doctrine of grace allowed him to realize that the *obedientia passiva* could be, and, in fact, was transformed by means of its association with ascetic penitential practices into simply another, although more subtle, form of works-righteousness and meritoriousness. Luther had come to see that salvation is not brought about as a result of suffering and bearing the cross. Rather, it is freely offered by means of Christ's sacrificial death. Our faith in Christ is all that is required of us. This development in turn forms the basis of another part of Luther's doctrine of works -- namely, his belief that faith, not obedience, is the

159

primary requirement of the Christian life. It is faith that conforms us to the image of Christ.

From the point of view of one who was in dispute with an entire medieval worldview concerning the role and function of good works, Luther's development of *sola fide, sola gratia* was a significant, and no doubt, liberating assertion. It is nevertheless important to reexamine the roots of Luther's doctrine of faith in the *obedientia passiva* tradition of late medieval thought in order to understand properly why Luther's elaboration of his doctrine of faith and works was to take two clearly distinct and, in appearance, contradictory forms. While replacing *obedientia* with *fides*, Luther's understanding of faith retained the basic orientation or attitude in regard to faith which characterized the *obedientia passiva* tradition. His adoption of the notion of faith as passivity is precisely why Luther is forced into ambiguity and confusion in his elaboration of his doctrine of faith and works.

It may be slightly misleading to suggest that Luther simply replaced *obedientia* with *fides*, forming a *fides passiva* in line with the tradition of mystical theology and a *fides activa* in line with nominalism. Nevertheless, in his elaboration of the doctrine of faith and works, Luther does evoke two distinct conceptions which have much in common with the *passiva* and *activa* traditions. At times, Luther argues in support of a *fides abstracta* (or *fides absoluta*), an abstract, unfinished or unformed faith which is sufficient in and of itself.[29] However, at other times he argues in favour of a *fides incarnata*, which suggests that faith is in need of actualization and concretion (and, at times, validation) through the active expression of good works.[30] This inconsistency appears to be a continuation of his inability to resolve properly from the outset of his career the irreconcilable differences between the *obedientia activa* and *obedientia passiva* traditions which originally informed his thought.

It can now be argued that ultimately Luther did not choose between an active or passive interpretation of the life of faith. In his elaboration of his doctine of faith and good works, Luther approved both a *fides abstracta* and a *fides incarnata* at various times. Therefore, both those who find support for an active conception of the life of faith and those who see support for a passive conception of the life of faith in Luther's writings would be correct. However, to regard one and exclude the other as properly representing Luther's thought on the matter, would be arbitrary and illegitimate.[31]

It may be considered as inconsistent to hold to two distinctive interpretations of faith which in many senses are mutually exclusive. However, Luther was no systematic theologian and this is precisely what he concluded was required. Luther also believed that in advocating both a *fides abstracta* and a *fides incarnata* he had the support of Scripture.

> We also distinguish faith in this way, that sometimes faith is understood apart from the work and sometimes with the work. For just as a craftsman speaks about his material in different ways ..., so the Holy Spirit speaks about faith in different ways in Scripture: sometimes, if I may speak this way, about an abstract or an absolute faith and sometimes about a concrete, composite, or incarnate faith. Thus if Christ is looked at on the basis of outward appearance, He seems to be mere man. And yet Scripture sometimes speaks of Christ as God, and sometimes it speaks of Him as composite and incarnate.[32]

The various Christological affirmations correspond to Luther's dual interpretation of the life of faith. Nevertheless, the question of their individual proclamation still remains to be resolved.

In his commentary on Galatians 5:8 of 1535, Luther writes, "The Anabaptists have nothing in their entire teaching more impressive than the way they emphasize the example of Christ and the bearing of the cross," but, we must learn to distinguish "when Christ is proclaimed as a gift and when as an

Fides Abstracta, Fides Incarnata

example. Both forms of proclamation have their proper time; if this is not observed, the proclamation of salvation becomes a curse."[33] And what is the proper time? Luther explains further:

> To those who are afraid and have already been terrified by the burden of their sins, Christ the Saviour and the gift should be announced, not Christ the example and lawgiver. But to those who are smug and stubborn the example of Christ should be set forth, lest they use the Gospel as a pretext for the freedom of the flesh and thus become smug.[34]

It is through suffering, through our own bearing of the cross, that we are made 'conformable' to Christ, so that through faith, Christ can take form in the Christian, forcing the Christian to conform to himself, and aiding the faithful in the continuing struggle against the self-righteousness, pride and smugness of 'the Old Adam.' Good works performed in imitation of Christ will most certainly result in failure and despair. "What an example the Lord has placed before our eyes," writes Luther, "but we cannot equal it: our light is like a burning straw against the sun."[35] Similarly, in terms of suffering: "The extent of His agony, the intensity and bitterness of His sufferings, no one can comprehend; and if it exceeds our comprehension how much more does it exceed our ability to imitate or experience?"[36]

Although the result will surely be that of failure, nevertheless this is not to suggest that the imitation of the example of Christ and good works should be rejected and suffering avoided. The function of the imitation of Christ, as is the function of the law itself, is to lead us into inner conflict, death and hell -- not that we should perish, but that we will turn again to faith in Christ. It is our failure and despair which reminds us that we are and continue to be *simul iustus et peccator* "as long as flesh and blood remain."[37] It is our failure and despair which reminds us that our faith is weak and 'how much we are still lacking.' This realization forces us to turn again to the *Christus donum* and faith in the prior work of the *Christus sacramentum*.[38] Luther continues:

> Scripture presents Christ in two ways. First as a gift .... Secondly, Scripture presents Him as an example for us to imitate. But I will not let this Christ be presented to me as exemplar except at a time

of rejoicing, when I am out of reach of temptations (when I can hardly attain a thousandth part of His example), so that I may have a mirror in which to contemplate how much I am still lacking, lest I become smug. But in a time of tribulation I will not listen to or accept Christ except as a gift ....[39]

Luther took with utmost seriousness the injunction of faith, which demands that we humbly serve the needs of our neighbour, to the point of placing deeply held theological doctrines themselves at the service of the neighbour. If a particular theological assertion does not serve the deepest needs of the neighbour, then it is not the neighbour but the doctrine which must be rejected. The needs of the neighbour must be taken into account in the formulation and proclamation of theology itself.

To proclaim the imitation of Christ to those who are suffering is to place an unbearable burden upon them, which does not serve Christ or the neighbour. To proclaim the free gift of salvation to those who are smug leads to further self-righteousness, which again does not serve Christ or the neighbour. Only true faith, and a genuine desire to express that faith through our love for the neighbour, permits us to exclaim, albeit under different circumstances, both that good works are necessary and that good works are not necessary.

The appropriate Christological affirmations and concomitant doctrine of works are evoked in response to the demands of the historical context. Different situations and circumstances require a different proclamation of faith and works, but a proclamation which nevertheless has its source in the *sacramentum et exemplum* of the one reality of Jesus the Christ.

- 9 -

Luther was always at his best when engaged in polemics. The clarity of his earlier opponents in the Roman Church forced his own clarity whereas the variety and ambiguities among his later opponents obscures Luther's stance. The many-sided disputes, while in some cases leading Luther to over-defensive reactions, upon other occasions also led to his theological depth.

Luther's theology reflects the dynamics of his life, changing with the ever-changing demands of the historical situation, sometimes resulting in positions consistent with previous utterances while on other occasions inconsistent with previous positions. To some extent, at least in his later years, Luther appears to have become cognizant of these inconsistencies. Luther was not a systematic theologian and he makes little attempt to resolve the discrepancies, choosing instead to affirm both a *fides abstracta* and a *fides incarnata*. Both are valid depending upon the nature of the situation within which one finds oneself.

One of the more pronounced features arising out of the epistemological theory of the *via antiqua* tradition was the need to harmonize, synthesize or otherwise resolve contradictions. This, in part, may account for its tendencies toward theological and political centralization. Luther, with his roots in the decentralizing tendencies of the *via moderna* and the mystics' *via contrarii*, continuously juxtaposes antithetical or seemingly contradictory concepts as sharply as possible (e.g., *simul*, the two *solas*). Luther's paradoxical formulations represented, as with all paradox, the attempt to move beyond conceptual theology in order to point more clearly to the *Deus absconditus* hidden beneath contrary appearance.

The life of faith is lived in the midst of contradictions, not in their resolution, whether it be by a rationalization of discrepancies or by means of choosing among conflicting claims. The nature of faith is such that we are assured of God's grace on those occasions that we realize that we must change what we cannot accept, just as at those times that we realize that we must accept what we cannot change.

It is difficult to determine whether Luther was actually conscious of his use of two distinct interpretations of the life of faith, for except in the few places cited occurring toward the end of his career, the *fides abstracta* and *fides incarnata* are never maintained in the same statement. This makes it difficult to claim that Luther was intentionally establishing a paradoxical view of the nature of faith. It is more likely that Luther's theological methodology, which never sought to harmonize, synthesize or otherwise resolve contradictions and paradoxes, predisposed him to leaving discrepancies unresolved once he became aware of them.

Rather than seeing the inconsistency which characterizes Luther's understanding of the nature of faith as an inherent weakness of his thought, it may be viewed instead as one of his most significant legacies. For rather than trapping those who come after in the straits of confessional dogmatics Luther left a legacy of theological consciousness which in its ambiguity not only leaves room for, but demands that the theological enterprise be radically creative in each new historical circumstance and situation.

Here theology reveals itself as a continuing wayfaring and not as a rigid system, even if again and again it has to make affirmations which are 'systematic' (that is to say, rationally consistent and conceptually coherent in themselves). Luther left us with a paradoxical view of faith which corresponds to, and allows us to participate in, the essential paradox found at the very heart of Christianity itself -- Jesus Christ, fully human, fully Divine, suspended on a cross between heaven and earth.

NOTES

1. *LW* 34, p. 111; *WA* 39 I, p. 46; see also *WA* 32, p. 520; *LW* 31, p. 361; *LW* 26, p. 255; *WA* 40 I, p. 402.

2. *WA* 44, p. 135.

3. *LW* 35, p. 370.

4. *LW* 27, p. 96; *WA* 40 II, p. 121.

5. *WA* 40 II, p. 11 -- italics mine.

6. *LW* 35, p. 370; see also *LW* 27, p. 30; *WA* 40 II, p. 37; *WA* 12, p. 289.

7. *WA* 39 II, p. 248.

8. *LW* 34, p. 111; see also *WA* 40, p. 783; *WA* 39 II, p. 248; *WA* 40 II, p. 37; *LW* 27, p. 30.

9. *WA* 5, p. 407.

10. See Peter Manns, "Absolute and Incarnate Faith -- Luther on Justification in the Galatians' Commentary of 1531-1535," in *Catholic Scholars Dialogue with Luther*, ed. Jared Wicks (Chicago: Loyola University Press, 1970), p. 31; see also pp. 131-156, 205-223.

11. See Robert Bertram, "The Radical Dialectic Between Faith and Works in Luther's Lectures on Galatians (1535)," in *Luther for an Ecumentical Age: Essays in Commemoration of the 450th Anniversary of the Reformation*, ed. Carl S. Meyer (Saint Louis: Concordia Publishing House, 1967), pp. 219-241.

12. *Christus non curat politiam art oeconomiam -- WA Tr.* 1, p. 932.

13. *LW* 46, p. 35.

14. *WA* 40 I, p. 41.

15. *WA* 33, p. 566.

16. *LW* 26, p. 274; *WA* 40 I, p. 428. See Prenter, *Spiritus Creator*, p. 28.

17. *LW* 26, p. 270; *WA* 40 I, p. 424.

18. *LW* 26, p. 143.

19. *LW* 27, p. 25; *WA* 40 II, p. 29.

20. See Heinecken, "Luther and the 'Orders of Creation' in Relation to a Doctrine of Work and Vocation," p. 393.

21. *WA* 20, p. 641; *WA* 45, p. 701; *WA* 47, p. 114.

22. *WA* 40 I, p. 251.

23. *LW* 26, p. 155; *WA* 40 I, p. 266.

24. For a history of the period from 1546-1577 see T. R. Junghuntz, *Formulators of the Formula of Concord: Four Architects of Lutheran Unity* (Saint Louis: Concordia Publishing House, 1977), *passim.*

25. It was under the direction of Luther's old friend and colleague, Philipp Melanchthon, that the great compromise of Concord was attained to the satisfaction of most participants. Melanchthon was a product of the *via antiqua* tradition of which one of the more pronounced features was the need to harmonize, synthesize or otherwise resolve contradictions and paradoxes. Confessionalism and contradiction make strange bedfellows. An unforeseen by-product of Melanchthon's search for unity was to direct the Lutheran reformation toward a Protestant scholasticism. See L. W. Spitz and L. Lohff, eds., *Discord, Dialogue and Concord: Studies in the Lutheran Reformation's Formula of Concord* (Philadelphia: Fortress Press, 1977), *passim.*

26. Later Lutheran orthodoxy is often blamed for overemphasizing a *fides abstracta.* It is alleged that Luther's doctrine of faith and works is best expressed as a *fides incarnata* and Lutheran orthodoxy is at divergence from Luther in this regard. Walther von Loewenich, for example, claims that "Orthodoxy was totally concerned with emphasizing the all-sufficiency of Christ's sacrifice. For that reason it isolated the doctrine concerning Christ's work" (*Luther's Theology of the Cross*, p. 121; see also Prenter, "Luther's Theology of the Cross," pp. 226ff.).
   As has been shown however, one does not have to look to Melanchthon or Concord or the dogmaticians of Lutheran orthodoxy as misunderstanding or misrepresenting Luther's doctrine of faith and works. Luther as well emphasized a *fides abstracta* on occasion in his emphasis upon the all-sufficiency of Christ's sacrifice and his warnings against purposeful striving. In this sense, orthodoxy is not the illegitimate stepchild but legitimate heir of Luther's thought -- a fact that both Karlstadt and the Anabaptists were quick to recognize and criticize in both Luther and Lutherans.

27. A proponent of this position is Walther von Loewenich who writes that Luther, "matured by his battles for the Gospel and enriched by experiences, traded in (his) negatively defined concept of faith for a positive one and began to stress in connection with faith, the present possession rather than the expectancy of future blessings. The quietistic elements of faith give way to the activistic, the world-shunning elements give way to those that shape the world" (*Luther's Theology of the Cross*, pp. 84-85).

28. *LW* 26, p. 274; *WA* 40 I, p. 428.

29. The terms are Luther's own -- see *LW* 26, pp. 264ff.; *WA* 40 I, pp. 414ff.; and *LW* 10, p. 435; *WA* 3, p. 495.

30. Regin Prenter points out that "Our language does not have a word which directly expresses the unity of faith and love (religion and morals) which is fundamental to Luther" (*Spiritus Creator*, p. 64, fn. 53). Whereas Prenter suggests the term 'piety' to convey this unity, our discussion will employ the term *fides incarnata*, as did Luther (*LW* 26, p. 272; *WA* 40 I, p. 427) in order to convey a sense of the external focus of an internal faith. It is hoped that the connotation evoked by the term 'piety,' which historically has manifested itself in movements where moral behaviour was determined more by societal norms than faith, will thereby be avoided.

31. In *Faith Victorious*, Lennart Pinomaa writes, "With Christ as our example we end up in despair; as God's gift to us He is our life and salvation" (p. 49). This analysis is clearly in keeping with Luther's statements in support of a *fides abstracta* position. However, the implications drawn from this analysis are not at all what Luther intended. Luther does not suggest we avoid suffering and despair or reject good works or the imitation of Christ. The choice is not "*Christus sacramentum* or *Christus exemplum*" as Pinomaa maintains (p. 49). Luther's stance has more in common with the mystics' *simul* than with existential choices.

32. *LW* 26, p. 264; *WA* 40 I, p. 414.

33. *LW* 27, p. 35.

34. *Ibid.*

35. *WA* 15, p. 497.

36. *WA* 21, p. 300.

37. *LW* 30, p. 70; *WA* 12, p. 326.

38. *LW* 27, p. 86.

39. *Ibid.*, p. 34.

***

NAME INDEX

à Kempis. See *Thomas à Kempis*
Abelard, Peter 23
Anselm 97, 103, 104
Aquinas, Thomas.
  See *Thomas Aquinas*
Aristotle 22, 23, 34, 41
Augustine of Hippo 12, 21, 29-33,
  36-38, 40, 41, 48, 57, 58, 75,
  93-95, 99, 102, 105, 159
Bernard of Clairvaux 13, 22, 40, 49-
  53, 57, 58, 63, 69, 70, 78, 89,
  93, 102, 149
Biel, Gabriel 16-28, 30-33, 35-40,
  43, 44, 47, 49, 53, 56-59, 61,
  67, 70, 88, 93, 96, 141, 159
Charles V 119
Cusa. See *Nicholas of Cusa*
d'Ailly, Peter 16, 88
d'Étaples, Jacques Léfèvre.
  See *Stapulensis*
Denck, Hans 134, 147
Dionysius the Areopagite 77
Eckhart. See *Meister Eckhart*
Franck, Sebastian 150
Gansfort, Wesel 88
Gerson, Jean 16, 39, 53, 70, 115
Grebel, Conrad 150
Gregory of Rimini 16, 32, 33, 40,
  41, 109
Groote, Gerhard 88
Hubmaier, Balthasar 135, 145, 148
Jerome 23
John XXII 23, 32, 88
Karlstadt. See *von Karlstadt*
Major, Georg 1, 4, 5, 9, 76, 156
Meister Eckhart 75, 77, 78, 80, 88

Melanchthon, Philipp 118, 147, 167
Müntzer, Thomas 126, 145-148, 150
Nicholas of Cusa 71
Ockham. See *William of Ockham*
Pelagius 30, 31, 40
Philip of Hesse 133
Pinomaa, Lennart 3-7, 98, 99, 101,
  102, 104, 168
Prenter, Regin 3-5, 7, 91, 92, 104,
  149, 166-168
Pseudo-Dionysius.
  See *Dionysius the Areopagite*
Radewijns, Florens 88
Rink, Melchior 134
Schwenckfeld, Caspar 135, 147
Scotus, John Duns 9, 12-14, 21, 33,
  36
Spalatin, Georg 113
Stapulensis, Jacobus Faber 53-61, 63,
  68, 70, 71, 75, 76, 83, 93, 110
Storch, Nicholas 119
Tarvainen, Olavi 3-7
Tauler, Johannes 39, 71, 75-87, 89,
  90, 93, 127, 128, 131
Tetzel, Johann 106
Thomas à Kempis 43, 71
Thomas Aquinas 10, 12-14, 21-23
Trutvetter, Jodocus 16, 25
van Ruysbroeck, Jan 75
von Amsdorf, Nickolaus 156
von Goch, Johannes Popper 88
von Karlstadt, Andreas Bodenstein
  73, 118-130, 135-137, 153-155,
  157, 167
von Loewenich, Walther 23, 71, 73,
  89-91

SUBJECT INDEX

Jena 126, 130

law 4, 5, 11-13, 21, 65, 95, 99, 101, 104, 123, 128, 135, 136, 139, 140, 143, 145, 147, 148, 152, 162. See also *lex naturalis, tertius usus legis*

legalism 139, 142, 145

Leipzig 118, 127

lex naturalis 11

literalism 54, 139, 145

Lutheran 7, 23, 40, 69, 105, 128, 129, 133, 134, 136, 146-148, 156, 167. See also *Gnessio-Lutherans*

Manichaeaism 31, 36

Mennonites 131. See also *Anababtists*

meritoriousness, *meritum* 3, 5, 15, 46, 57, 96, 102, 112-114, 123, 137, 159

   meritum de condigno 15

   meritum de congruo 15

monasticism 44, 45

mystica incarnatio 86

mystical theology 18, 50, 52, 54, 71, 73, 76, 80, 89, 93, 121, 131, 159, 160. See also *mystica incarnatio, mysticism, unio mystica*

mysticism 3-5, 22, 49, 50, 52, 58, 63, 66, 67, 70, 71, 74, 76, 77, 79, 80, 82, 86, 89-91, 93, 105, 128, 142, 145, 146, 148. See also *mystica incarnatio, mystical theology, unio mystica*

nachfolgen, nachfolgung 49, 89

   nachfolge Christi 7, 135

nominalist, nominalists, nominalism 9, 14-17, 22, 23, 39, 52, 53, 55, 67, 70, 93, 159, 160

obedience, *obedientia* 4, 20, 21, 44, 45, 56-60, 63, 93, 96, 129, 139, 159, 160

   obedientia activa 20, 21, 44, 45, 56, 57, 59, 93, 159, 160

obedientia passiva 56-60, 63, 93, 159, 160

Obenites 131

Ockhamist, Ockhamists, Ockhamism 14-19, 23, 25, 26, 28, 29, 31, 32, 39, 41, 65, 115

opus Dei

   opus alienum Dei 62, 64, 66

   opus proprium Dei 62, 64, 66

   opus suum Dei 65, 76

ordo salutis 82, 124

Orlamünde 126, 128

Paul 33, 53, 54, 57, 63, 71, 81, 85, 90, 93, 99, 105, 117, 134, 137, 149

peccator 35, 57, 60, 61, 87, 92, 101, 147, 162

peccatum 19, 20, 35, 62, 96

   peccatum originale 20, 35, 96

Pelagianism 31, 32, 34

Peter 16, 25, 38, 52, 88, 99, 105, 148, 166

Philippians 110, 116

pneumatology 130, 142, 143, 145. See also *Holy Spirit*

potentia 12, 27, 109

   potentia Dei absoluta 12

Psalms 25, 33, 53, 70, 71, 75, 94

purgation 55, 58, 59, 63, 82

rationis 11, 13, 14, 18, 19, 24, 26, 56, 67, 93, 100. See also *conformitas voluntatis et rationis Dei*

resignatio 50, 55, 56, 58-60, 71, 82-84

   resignatio voluntatis 50, 55, 56, 58-60, 71, 82-84

righteousness 3, 5, 10, 11, 15, 20, 33-35, 39, 42, 44-48, 56, 57, 59-61, 66, 67, 81-87, 96, 97, 99, 100, 109, 111-114, 123, 125, 134, 137, 138, 141, 148, 151, 154, 159, 162, 163

Romans 33, 36, 46, 53, 63, 65, 94, 103

Subject Index

sacramentum 5, 6, 20, 40, 93-105,
  108, 109, 111, 114, 140, 153,
  157, 162, 163, 168. See also
  Christus sacramentum
  sacramentum et exemplum 5, 40,
  93-96, 98-100, 103-105, 108,
  157, 163
salvation 10, 11, 20, 21, 30-35, 37,
  42-44, 47, 55, 56, 59-65, 67,
  82, 83, 87, 94, 95, 97, 98,
  100, 101, 106-108, 111, 112,
  123, 132, 134, 154, 156, 159,
  162, 163, 168. See also
  soteriology, ordo salutis
sanctification 89, 90, 121, 131-134
satisfaction 97, 132, 134, 135, 167
Saxony 48, 126
scholasticism 3, 9, 10, 12, 23, 25,
  30, 35-37, 44, 49, 50, 52, 57,
  58, 73, 79, 93, 131, 134, 139,
  142, 151, 167
Seelengrund 50, 78
similitudo 55, 79, 84, 85, 101
simul iustus et peccator 87, 162
sin 4, 5, 19, 20, 22, 23, 30, 31,
  33-35, 37, 50, 57, 58, 60, 62,
  67, 81, 83, 86, 96, 97, 99,
  111, 124, 129, 132, 141, 142,
  148, 159. See also *peccator,
  peccatum, peccatum originale,
  simul iustus et peccator*
sola fide 4, 84, 96, 98, 101, 102,
  106, 107, 110, 113-115, 125,
  126, 134, 136, 146, 153-155,
  157, 160. See also *faith, fides,
  fides absoluta, fides abstracta,
  fides Christi, fides incarnata*
  sola fides justificat 113, 122, 135
sola gratia 4, 62, 67, 81, 82, 84, 96,
  98, 101, 102, 107, 110,
  113-115, 125, 126, 134, 136,
  157, 159, 160. See also *gratia*
sola scriptura 139, 148
soteriology 5, 6, 112, 124, 138. See
  also *salvation, ordo salutis*

spiritualists 130, 141, 143, 145, 150,
  155, 157
stations 120, 121, 127, 128
Strassburg 126
synteresis 12-15, 18-23, 26-29,
  31-33, 35-37, 39, 42, 44, 45,
  48, 50, 56, 57, 59, 61, 78, 79,
  82-84, 86, 87, 95, 98, 131,
  141, 142
  synteresis rationis 13, 14, 18
  synteresis voluntatis et rationis
  18, 19, 26
tertius usus legis 139, 148. See also
  law, legalism, lex naturalis
theologia crucis 63, 73, 76, 89, 100,
  110, 121, 122
theologia Germanica 89
theologia gloriae 73, 85
unio mystica 51, 77-79, 90, 91. See
  also *mysticism, mystical
  theology, mystica incarnatio*
viae 9-11, 14-16, 39, 70, 138
  via antiqua 9, 11, 13, 15, 17-19,
  22, 41, 52, 164, 167
  via contrarii 62, 63, 83, 164
  via Gregorii 32, 41
  via moderna 9, 15-17, 22, 25,
  164
Vienna 16, 119
vocation, *vocatio* 4, 7, 120, 127,
  128, 166. See also *Beruf,
  calling*
will, *voluntas* 4-6, 8, 11, 12, 14, 15,
  17-22, 27, 28, 30-32, 34-38,
  44, 46, 47, 51, 52, 55-66, 68,
  71, 73, 75-78, 80, 82, 83, 96,
  101, 107, 112, 117, 119, 121,
  128, 129, 132-134, 136, 138-
  145, 147-149, 154, 159, 162,
  163, 168. See also *free will*
Wittenberg 17, 25, 32, 38, 48, 118,
  119, 125, 126, 128, 129, 133
works 1, 3, 5, 6, 10, 11, 13, 15,
  18-22, 27, 32-35, 37, 40, 43-
  49, 51, 54, 56, 57, 60, 62, 63,

174

65, 81, 82, 95, 96, 98, 99,
101, 102, 105-116, 120, 121,
122-126, 132-145, 148, 149,
151-163, 166-168. See also
good works

works-righteousness 46, 48, 57,
60, 96, 99, 113, 114, 123,
125, 134, 137, 138, 148, 159

Worms 41, 42, 69, 126

Zürich 119, 146

Zwickau prophets 121, 149

TEXTS AND STUDIES IN RELIGION

34. Samuel J. Rogal, **John Wesley's London: A Guidebook 1738-1791**

35. André Séguenny, **The Christology of Caspar Schwenckfeld: Spirit and Flesh in the Process of Life Transformation,** Peter C. Erb and Simone S. Nieuwolt (trans.)

36. Donald E. Demaray, **The Innovation of John Newton (1725-1807): Synergism of Word and Music in Eighteenth Century Evangelism**

37. Thomas Chase, **The English Religious Lexis**

38. R.G. Moyles, **A Bibliography of Salvation Army Literature in English 1865-1987**

39. Vincent A. Lapomarda, **The Jesuits and the Third Reich**

40. Susan Drain, **The Anglican Church in the 19th Century Britain: Hymns Ancient and Modern (1860-1875)**

41. Aegidius of Rome, **On Ecclesiastical Power: De Ecclesiastica Potestate,** Arthur P. Monahan (trans.)

42. John R. Eastman, **Papal Abdication in Later Medieval Thought**

43. Paul Badham (ed.), **Religion, State, and Society in Modern Britain**

44. Hans Denck, **Selected Writings of Hans Denck, 1500-1527,** E. J. Furcha (trans.)

45. Dietmar Lage, **Martin Luther on the** Imitatio Christi **and** Conformitas Christi **and Their Relationship To Good Works**

46. Jean Calvin, Sermons on Jeremiah by Jean Calvin, Blair Reynolds (trans.)

47. Jean Calvin, Sermons on Micah by Jean Calvin, Blair Reynolds (trans.)

48. Alexander Sándor Unghváry, **The Hungarian Protestant Reformation in the Sixteenth Century Under the Ottoman Impact: Essays and Profiles**

49. Daniel B. Clendenin & W. David Buschart (ed.), **Scholarship, Sacraments and Service: Historical Studies in Protestant Tradition** Essays in Honor of Bard Thompson